William Howard Doane

The Little Sunbeam

William Howard Doane

The Little Sunbeam

ISBN/EAN: 9783337334871

Printed in Europe, USA, Canada, Australia, Japan

Cover: Foto ©Thomas Meinert / pixelio.de

More available books at **www.hansebooks.com**

THE

LITTLE SUNBEAM;

A COLLECTION OF MUSIC,

CONSISTING OF

CHORUSES, QUARTETTES, TRIOS, CHANTS, ETC.

FOR SABBATH SCHOOLS, &c.

By W. H. DOANE.

CINCINNATI:

PUBLISHED BY J. CHURCH, JR., 66 W. FOURTH ST.

1867.

PREFACE.

THIS little work is not designed, in any sense, to be a rival or competitor to any Sabbath School book, but a friendly Co-operater to all. It has been the wish of the Author to make it a work of intrinsic value to every Sabbath School in America. In preparing this work he has aimed to seek for songs, as far as could be, that would impress the duty of cheerful submission to the Daily Cross, and the daily trials that are doubtless apportioned to each, as a part of needful discipline. Believing that it is not so much the *number* of the pieces named in the index, that contributes the desideratum, as the appropriateness of those that are presented, the Author has refrained from filling occasional pages with words to be sung to tunes in other parts of the book. He has endeavored to furnish a small but valuable collection of Sabbath School Music, at such a price as to enable all Sabbath Schools to supply themselves with it, in addition to the regular Music Book already in use, with but trifling additional expense. It is believed that this plan will place this little work within the reach of all Classes of Sabbath Schools, particularly *Mission Schools,* and those of destitute regions; in fact, all who are unable to provide more costly ones. Every song will be found a gem, and it is prayerfully hoped that it may not only be a welcome guest, but may, indeed, under God, prove a "Sun-beam" to warm the heart of every one with love to Christ, and be the means of leading them to "*Cling to that Rock which is higher than they.*"

W. H. DOANE.

GENERAL INDEX.

THE LITTLE SUNBEAM.

WAITING BY THE RIVER.

Arr. by W. H. D.

DUET.—*Repeat first verse Full Chorus.*

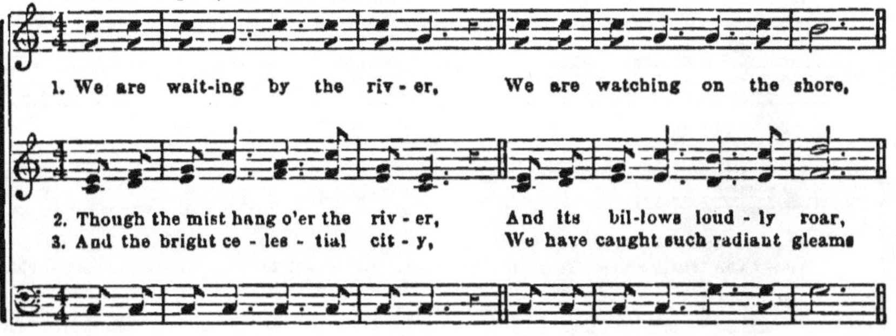

1. We are wait-ing by the riv - er, We are watching on the shore,
2. Though the mist hang o'er the riv - er, And its bil-lows loud - ly roar,
3. And the bright ce - les - tial cit - y, We have caught such radiant gleams

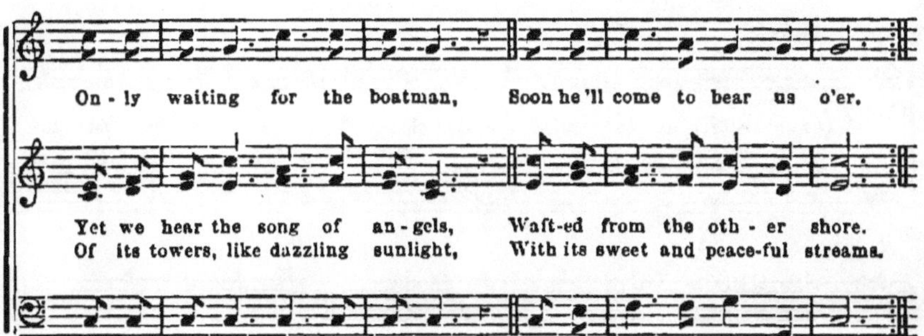

On - ly waiting for the boatman, Soon he'll come to bear us o'er.
Yet we hear the song of an - gels, Waft-ed from the oth - er shore.
Of its towers, like dazzling sunlight, With its sweet and peace-ful streams.

4 He has called for many a loved one,
We have seen them leave our side;
With our Savior we shall meet them,
When we too have crossed the tide.
We are waiting, etc.

5 When we've passed that vale of shadows,
With its dark and chilling tide;
In that bright and glorious city
We shall evermore abide.
We are waiting, etc.

THE LITTLE SOLDIER.

W. H. Doane.

Lively.

1. I'm going to be a sol - dier, Gird on my ar - mor bright, And with my lit - tle
2. The foes that will as - sail me Are subtle, fierce, and strong, The war that they are

comrades, I'll take the field and fight; I'll nev - er mind the hard-ship, Nor
wag-ing, Will dead - ly be and long; But I've a well-tried hel - met, A

dan-ger in the way, I'll watch, and toil, and wrestle, By night as well as day.
sword and trusty shield, To quench the fie-ry ar - rows, That Sa-tan's band may wield.

Chorus.

I'll nev - er, nev - er mind the hard-ships, I'll nev - er, nev - er fear the
way, For Je - sus is my Cap - tain, and I am sure to win.

3 I know I'm small and feeble,
But Jesus is my head,
He is wise and strong and able—
To triumph he will lead;
And when beneath his banner,
I've gained the victor's crown,
With one long, loud hosanna,
I'll lay my armor down.

WE HAVE MET IN LOVE TOGETHER.

Words by W. G. Clarke. Music by W. H. Doane.

1. We have met in love to - geth - er, In our Sun - day-school a - gain;

2. We have met, and time is fly - ing; We shall part, and still his wing,
3. He will aid us, should ex - ist - ence With its sor - rows sting the breast;

Constant friends have led us hith - er, Here to chant the sol - emn strain;

Sweeping o'er the dead and dy - ing, Will the change-ful sea - sons bring.
Gleaming in the on - ward distance, Faith will mark the land of rest.

Here to breathe our a - dor - a - tion, Here the Sav - ior's praise to sing;

Let us, while our hearts are light - est, In our fresh and ear - ly years,
There, midst day-beams round him playing, We our Fa - ther's face shall see,

May the spir - it of sal - va - tion Come with heal - ing in his wings.

Turn to Him whose smile is brightest, And whose grace will calm our fears.
And shall hear him gent - ly say - ing, "Lit-tle chil-dren, come to me."

WE'LL SING IN HEAVEN.

Words by J. R. OSGOOD. Music by W. H. DOANE.

1. We love to think of heaven a - bove, That ho - ly, bless-ed land,
2. We love to sing of heaven a - bove, That beau - ti - ful a - bode

3. We love to talk of heaven a - bove, How joy - ful it will be
4. We love to read of heaven a - bove, Its harps and crowns of gold,
5. We love to hope for heaven a - bove, Where sin nor death can come,

Where all the good shall gath-ered be, A lov - ing, hap - py band.
Of chil - dren saved by Je - sus' blood, The dwell-ing-place of God.

When we shall join the ser - aph songs, Their glorious minds shall see.
Its jas - per walls and pearl - y gates, Its joys and bliss un - told.
Where we shall join those gone be - fore, In Christ, our Sav - ior's home.

Chorus. *f*

We'll sing in heaven, sing in heaven, Round the throne in glo - ry;

We'll sing in heaven, sing in heaven, Round the throne in glo - ry;

ff
We'll join the ar - my of the Lord, Who all will meet in heaven.

DOING SOMETHING FOR CHRIST.

W. H. DOANE.

Allegro.
1. If you can not in the pul - pit, Preach the Word with flowing zeal,
Tell-ing of the love of Je - sus, Caus-ing mul - ti - - - - tudes to feel,
D. C. Meet a - mong the high and low - ly, Spreading forth the Gospel rule.
2. If you can not, in the jun - gle, Far in for - eign lands a-way,
Teach the poor, be-night-ed heath-en To forsake their - - sins and pray;
D. C. You can aid the mis-sion - a - ry Thus to chris-tian-ize their mind.
D. C.
You can on the Lord's day, ho - ly, In the pleas-ant Sab - bath school,
You can send the means to help them The pure light of truth to find;
Chorus.
O! then, be up and do - ing now— Do - ing some good work for the Lord;
O! then, be up and do - ing now— Do - ing some good work for the Lord.
Ev - er in your path-way strew - ing, Ho - ly pre - cepts from his Word.
Ev - er in your path-way strew - ing, Ho - ly pre - cepts from his Word.

3 O! then, pray be up and doing
Some good work for Christ, the Lord;
Ever in your pathway strewing
Holy precepts from his Word;
That some poor benighted creatures
May their evil ways forsake,
And from Christ the Lord, the Giver,
His own righteousness partake.
O! then, pray, etc.

4 Then you can look forward, happy
In the thought of doing good—
Hear the welcome plaudit given,
"You my words have understood;
You have truly preached my Gospel,
You have now proclaimed my Word;
You have been a true disciple;
Now rejoice in Christ your Lord."
O! then, pray, etc.

I LONG TO CROSS OVER.

Music by W. H. Doane.

1. O, have you not heard of that realm of delight, To which our blest Savior doth each one invite;
2. 'T is a land of rare beauty—a realm of delight, O'erflowing with gladness, refulgent with light;
3. There the weary may rest, and the wicked ne'er come; There the saints are all safe in their heavenly [home.
4. 'T is Jesus invites me this glory to see, To reign with him ever, all happy and free;
'T is prepared for the good and the pure and the blest, 'T is over the river where the weary find rest.
Its verdure ne'er withers, its flowers ne'er die, O, I long to cross over with Jesus on high.
With their harps and their crowns they forever are seen, Away o'er the river where the valleys are green.
I 'll join with the ransomed and with them abide, I 'll cross the dark river--bright angels will guide.
Chorus.
O, I long to cross over, And join the glad angels on Eden's fair plain!
O, I long to cross over, O, I long to cross over, And join the glad angels on Eden's fair plain!
O, I long to cross over, Yes, over the river with Jesus to reign!
O, I long to cross over, O, I long to cross over, Yes, over the river with Jesus to reign!

ONWARD, ONWARD, MARCH AND SING.

Words by J. M. LYON. Music by W. H. DOANE.

Lively.

1. On - ward, on - ward, sons of heaven, Haste ye for the thick - est fight;
2. Rise, nor yield to life - less slumbers; Buck - le on your ar - mor bright;
3. Long in pain and anguish groaning, Na - ture shall ere - long be free;

Ho - ly trusts to you are giv - en, Struggling ev - er for the right.
Face your foes, nor heed their num - bers, Strong in God - im - part - ed might.
Still for aye the cap - tives moaning, Blessed with God-born lib - er - ty.

See! the world is in com - mo - tion; Strange events and grand are nigh;
Dark is now the cloud of bat - tle; Loud the sounds of bit - ter strife;
Sol - dier, hark! from star - ry port - als Sound there words of love di - vine:

Ye, who of - fer true de - vo - tion, Lo! your Prince is pass - ing by.
Soon shall hush their din and rat - tle; Earth shall know a bet - ter life.
"Firm till death!" then bright immor - tals, Victors' wreaths each brow shall twine.

Chorus.

On - ward! on - ward! march and sing! Glo - ry! glo - ry
to our King! Glo - ry! glo - ry! Je - sus is our King!

SHALL WE MEET EACH OTHER THERE?

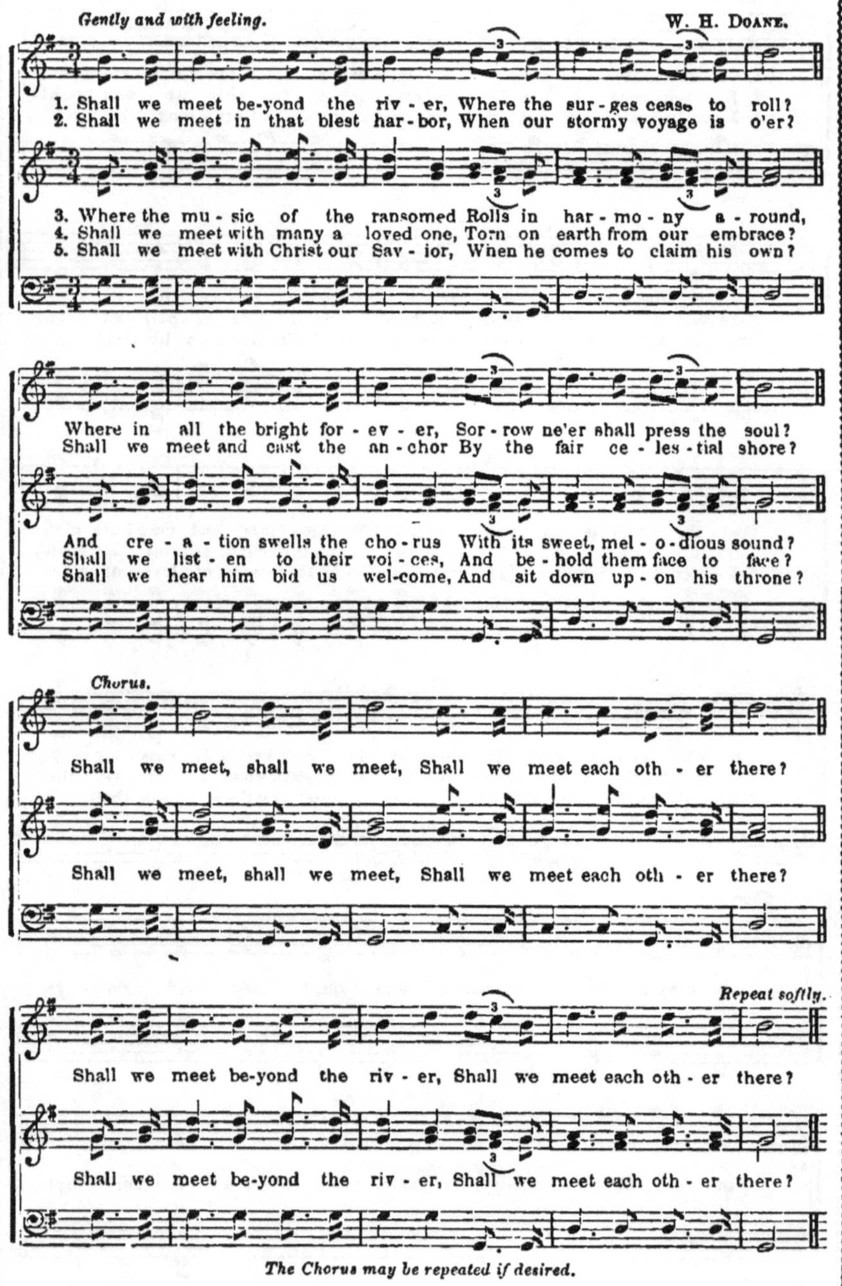
Gently and with feeling.
W. H. DOANE.
1. Shall we meet be-yond the riv - er, Where the sur - ges cease to roll?
2. Shall we meet in that blest har-bor, When our stormy voyage is o'er?
3. Where the mu - sic of the ransomed Rolls in har - mo - ny a - round,
4. Shall we meet with many a loved one, Torn on earth from our embrace?
5. Shall we meet with Christ our Sav - ior, When he comes to claim his own?
Where in all the bright for - ev - er, Sor - row ne'er shall press the soul?
Shall we meet and cast the an - chor By the fair ce - les - tial shore?
And cre - a - tion swells the cho - rus With its sweet, mel - o - dious sound?
Shall we list - en to their voi - ces, And be - hold them face to face?
Shall we hear him bid us wel-come, And sit down up - on his throne?
Chorus.
Shall we meet, shall we meet, Shall we meet each oth - er there?
Shall we meet, shall we meet, Shall we meet each oth - er there?
Repeat softly.
Shall we meet be-yond the riv - er, Shall we meet each oth - er there?
Shall we meet be-yond the riv - er, Shall we meet each oth - er there?

The Chorus may be repeated if desired.

"CLINGING TO THE ROCK."

W. H. DOANE.

Allegro.
1. When the tempest rages high, Sailing on life's bolsterous sea; Stormy billows I de-
2. When 'mid drifting wrecks I 'm cast, Darkness settling thickly round, Hope shall lift her
flight at
3. When the conquering waves shall close Proudly o'er me as I die; Over these brief victor
Chorus.
fy If I then may on - ly be Clinging to the Rock, Clinging to the Rock.
last, If I then be on - ly found Clinging to the Rock, Clinging to the Rock.
foes, I shal triumph while I cry, Clinging to the Rock, Clinging to the Rock.
Shel-ter for me ev-er, Strength that faileth never; When the storms of life are o'er,
Shel-ter for me ev-er, Strength that faileth never; When the storms of life are o'er,
Look for me on Canaan's shore, Clinging to the Rock, Clinging to the Rock.
Look for me on Canaan's shore, Clinging to the Bock, Clinging to the Rock.

HEAVENLY HOME, SWEET HOME.

Words by Miss J. W. Sampson. Music by W. H. Doane.

1. Heaven - ly home, heaven - ly home, Precious name to me; I

2. Heaven - ly home, heaven - ly home, There no clouds a - rise; No
3. Heaven - ly home, heaven - ly home, Ne'er shall sorrow's gloom, No

love to think the time will come When I shall rest in thee. I've no a - bid-ing cit - y here, I

tear-drops fall, no dark nights dim Thy ever-smiling skies. This earthly home is fair and bright, Yet
doubts nor fears disturb me there, For all is peace at home. I know I ne'er shall worthy be To

seek for one to come; And tho' my pil-grim-age be drear, I know there 's rest at home.

clouds will often come, And O, I long to see the light That gilds my heavenly home.
dwell 'neath heav'n's bright dome; But Christ my Savior died for me, And now he calls me home.

Chorus. *Repeat Chorus.*

Heavenly home, sweet home, Heavenly home, sweet home, Precious name to me, Home, sweet home.

Heaven - ly home, Heaven - ly home, Precious name to me, Home, sweet home.

Heavenly home, sweet home, Heavenly home, sweet home, Precious name to me, Home, sweet home.

WHO BUT JESUS?

Written expressly for the "Star Mission Sabbath-school," and respectfully inscribed to H. H. Shipley.

Music by W. H. Doane.

1. When the heart is bowed in sad - ness, Drooping like some blighted flower;
2. When with tear - ful eye re - view - ing Homes for - ev - er passed a - way;
3. When the storms of life o'ertake us, Raging fierce and long and loud;
4. In all darkness, in all dan - gers, In all sea - sons of dis - tress;
5. Je - sus, ev - er bless - ed Je - sus, Sweetest all of names for love;
Brightening to no smile of glad - ness, Cheered by no re - freshing shower—
Fond one's pathway ev - er strew - ing With love tok - ens day by day—
Friends and hopes alike for - sake us, No bright rainbow in the cloud—
'Mid this wil - der-ness as stran - gers, Wandering in heart lone - li - ness—
From all sin, all sor - row free us, Let us all thy friendship prove.
Chorus.
Who but Jesus then can cheer, Weary though each heart may be? Who but Jesus then can
Who but Jesus then can cheer, Weary though each heart may be? Who but Jesus then can
cheer us, save and bless? Who but Jesus then can cheer us, save and bless?
cheer us, save and bless? Who but Jesus then can cheer us, save and bless?

"CHRIST FOR ME."

W. H. DOANE.

1. My heart is fixed, E - ter - nal God, Fixed on thee; fixed on thee!
2. Let oth - ers boast of heaps of gold, Christ for me; Christ for me!

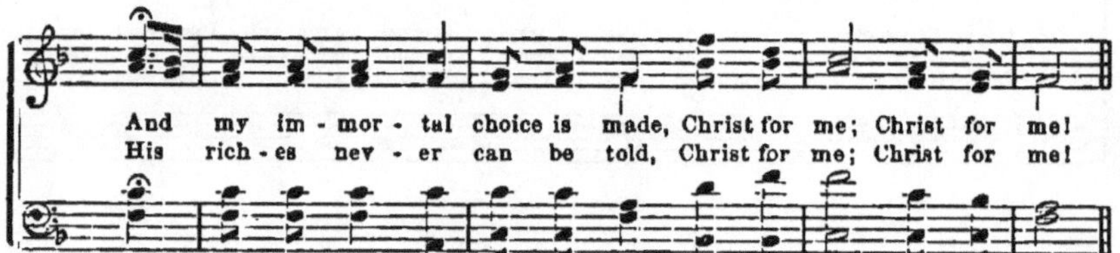
And my im - mor - tal choice is made, Christ for me; Christ for me!
His rich - es nev - er can be told, Christ for me; Christ for me!

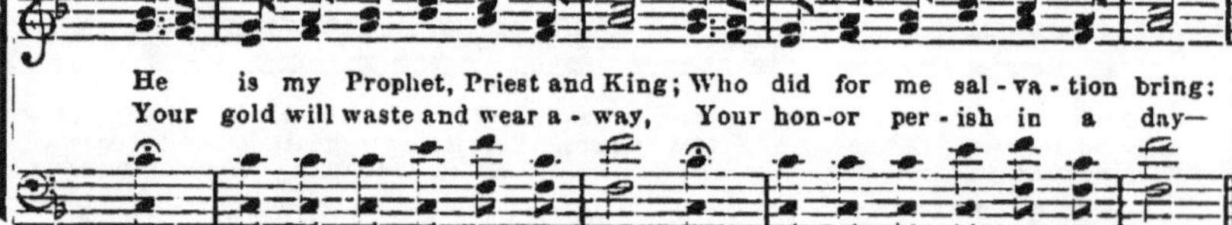
He is my Prophet, Priest and King; Who did for me sal - va - tion bring:
Your gold will waste and wear a - way, Your hon-or per - ish in a day—

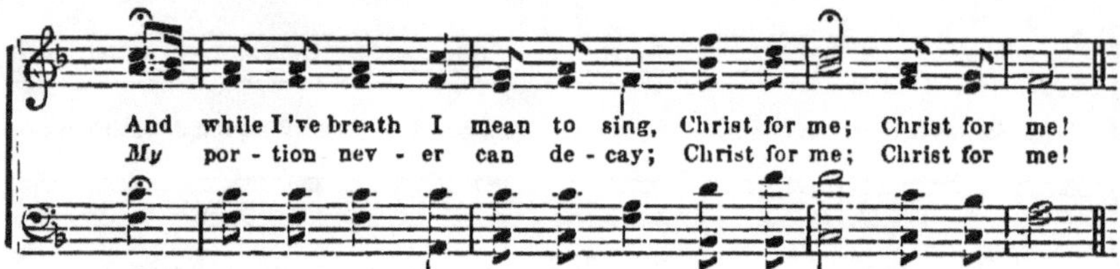
And while I've breath I mean to sing, Christ for me; Christ for me!
My por - tion nev - er can de - cay; Christ for me; Christ for me!

3 In pining sickness or in health,
Christ for me; Christ for me!
In deepest poverty or wealth,
Christ for me; Christ for me!
And in that all important day,
When I the summons must obey,
And pass from this dark world away,
Christ for me; Christ for me!

4 At home, abroad, by night and day,
Christ for me; Christ for me!
Whether I preach, or sing, or pray,
Christ for me; Christ for me!
Him first and last, him all day long,
My hope, my solace, and my song,
Convince me if you think I'm wrong—
Christ for me; Christ for me!

5 Now who can sing my song and say
Christ for me, Christ for me!
My light and truth, my life and way;
Christ for me; Christ for me!
Can you old man and woman say,
With furrowed cheeks and silvery hair,
Now from your inmost souls declare,
Christ for me; Christ for me!

6 Can you, young men and maidens, say
Christ for me; Christ for me!
Him will I love and him obey,
Christ for me; Christ for me!
Then here's my heart and here's my hand,
We'll form a happy singing band,
And shout aloud through all the land,
Christ for me; Christ for me!

I FEEL LIKE SINGING ALL THE TIME.

Little ELLA, one bright, beautiful Sabbath afternoon, exclaimed: "I think I have found the dear Jesus precious to my soul. The first time I came to the Sabbath-school I cried, but now *I feel like singing all the time.*"

Words by HAMMOND. Music by W. H. DOANE.

1. I feel like sing - ing all the time, My tears are wiped a - way;
2. When on the cross my Lord I saw, Nailed there with sins of mine,
3. When fierce tempt - a - tions try my heart, I'll sing of Je - sus divine;

For Je - sus is a friend of mine; I'll serve him ev' - ry day;
Fast fell the burn-ing tears, but now I'm sing - ing all the time;
And so, though tears at times may start, I'm sing - ing all the time;

I'll serve him ev' - ry day.
I'm sing-ing all the time.
I'm sing-ing all the time.

Chorus.

Sing - ing, sing - ing Glo - ry!

pp *Repeat.*

Sing - ing, sing-ing Glo - ry! glo - ry! Glo - ry be to God on high!

4 Oh, happy little singing one,
What music is like thine!
With Jesus as thy life and sun,
Go singing all the time;
Go singing all the time.
Singing, etc.

5 The melting story of the Lamb,
Tell with that voice of thine;
Till others with the glad "new song"
Go singing all the time;
Go singing all the time.
Singing, etc.

PRESS ON, LITTLE PILGRIMS.

Words by Rev. A. A. Graley. Music by W. H. Doane.

1. Press on, lit - tle pil-grims, and nev - er give up, Though oft - en your
2. Press on, lit - tle pil-grims, and lean on the Friend, Whose heart is the

3. Press on, lit - tle pil-grims, and nev - er re-treat, When Sa - tan comes
4. Press on, lit - tle pil-grims, your home is in view, Its doors are thrown

way may be drea - - - ry; Press on, lit - tle pil - grims, re-plen - ish your
em-pire of pit - - - y; Whose wis-dom can guide you, whose arm can de-

forth to an - noy - - you; The darts which he hurls with a mer - ci - less
wide to re - ceive - - you; A bright crown of glo - ry is laid up for

Chorus.

cup From wells of sal - va - tion when wea - ry. When you 've crossed the river,
fend, Till safe in the beau-ti - ful cit - y. When you 've, etc.

hate, May wound, but shall never de - stroy you. When you 've crossed the river,
you, And sor-row and sin will soon leave you. When you 've, etc.

You 'll be hap - py ev - er; Safe on Canaan's shore, You 'll be hap - py ev-er-more.

You 'll be hap-py ev - er; Safe on Canaan's shore, You 'll be hap-py ev-er-more.

HEAVY LADEN COME TO ME.

Words by C. C. — Music by W. H. DOANE.

1. Who is this that calls, "O, wear-y," Who is this that cries, "O, wear-y,"
2. Who is this that standeth wait-ing, Who is this so pa-tient wait-ing,
3. Who is this that go-eth weep-ing For the care-less heart is sleep-ing?
4. Who is this that prays "Forgive them," Who is this that pleads "Forgive them,"
Who is this that prays, "O, wea-ry, Hea-vy-la-den, come to me?"
Knocking, wait-ing, call-ing, wait-ing, Thro' the dark and storm-y night?
Who is this that go-eth weep-ing, "I have called, ye would not hear?"
All-for-giv-ing prays, "For-give them, For they know not what they do?"
Is there rest from sor-row's sigh-ing? Is there life for sin-ners dy-ing?
"I will sup with thee," he say-eth, "O-pen un-to me," he pray-eth,
Lo! the Lord you have re-ject-ed, Christ, the Lord, despised, re-ject-ed!
It is Je-sus, plead-ing, cry-ing, It is Je-sus, bleed-ing, dy-ing;
It is Je-sus who is cry-ing, "Heavy-la-den, come to me."
It is Je-sus wait-eth, pray-eth, In the dark-ness waits the light.
Je-sus scorned, despised, re-ject-ed! When you call, O who will hear?
Dy-ing sin-ners, Christ is dy-ing— Must he die in vain for you?
Chorus.
Je-sus calls! will you come? Hea-vy-la-den, sin-ner come?
Je-sus calls! will you come, Come and go to the prom-ised land?

"COME THOU FOUNT OF EVERY BLESSING."

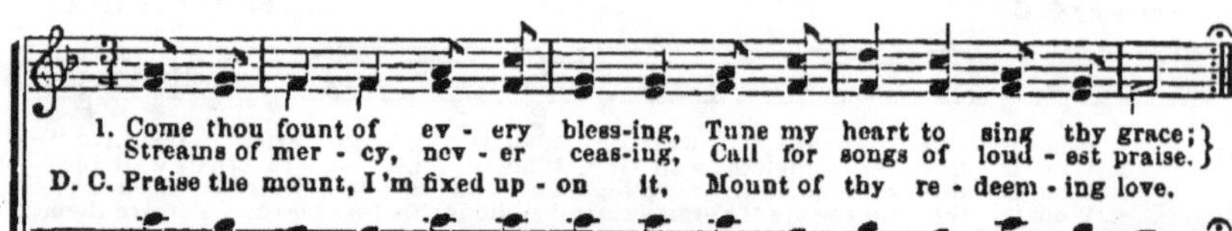
1. Come thou fount of ev - ery bless-ing, Tune my heart to sing thy grace;
Streams of mer - cy, nev - er ceas-ing, Call for songs of loud - est praise.
D. C. Praise the mount, I'm fixed up - on it, Mount of thy re - deem - ing love.

D. C.
Teach me some me - lo - dious son - net, Sung by flam-ing tongues a - bove;

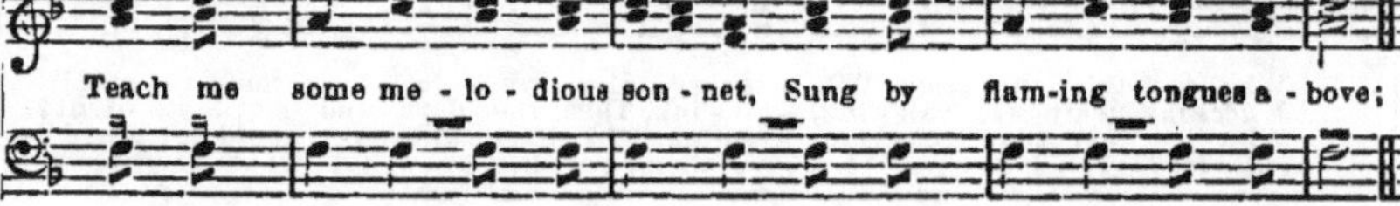

2 Here I raise my Ebenezer,
Hither by thy help I 'm come,
And I hope, by thy good pleasure,
Safely to arrive at home.
Jesus sought me when a stranger,
Wandering from the fold of God,
He, to rescue me from danger,
Interposed his precious blood.

3 O, to grace how great a debtor,
Daily I'm constrained to be!
Let thy goodness, like a fetter,
Bind my wandering heart to thee.
Prone to wander, Lord, I feel it,
Prone to leave the God I love,
Here 's my heart, O take and seal it
Seal it for thy courts above.

ROCK OF AGES, CLEFT FOR ME.

Dr. Hastings.

1. Rock of A - ges, cleft for me, Let me hide my-self in thee;
D. C. Be of sin a dou - ble cure, Save from wrath, and make me pure.

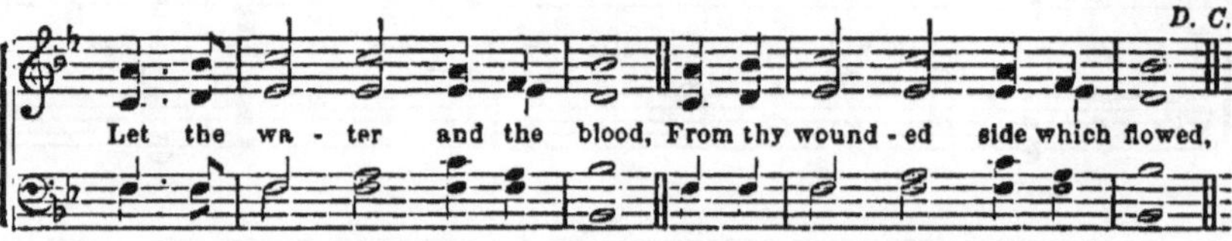
D. C.
Let the wa - ter and the blood, From thy wound - ed side which flowed,

2 Could my tears forever flow,
Could my zeal no languor know,
This for sin could not atone,
Thou must save, and thou alone;
In my hand no price I bring,
Simply to thy cross I cling.

While I draw this fleeting breath,
When my eyes shall close in death,
When I rise to worlds unknown,
And behold thee on thy throne,
Rock of Ages, cleft for me,
Let me hide myself in thee.

THEN, CHILDREN, SING AWAY.

Music by W. H. Doane.

Slow and softly, with expression.

1. Round the throne in glory Happy children throng, And redemption's story Wakes the harp and song.
2. Robes of snowy whiteness, Beautiful and rare; Crowns of radiant brightness, Such those children wear.

3. Now the skillful fingers Sweep the golden lyre; Not a harper lingers In that ransomed choir.
4. Children now sojourning In a world of sin, From your follies turning, Strive to enter in.

On the verdant mountain, By the shining stream Of the living fountain, Jesus is their theme.
Safe from death's bereavement, Sorrow, and the grave, Free from sin's enslavement, Victory's Palm they [wave.

Voices sweetly blending With the tuneful string, To the throne ascending, Praise the heavenly King.
Let your young affections Round the Savior twine, And 'mid heaven's attractions You shall sing and shine.

Chorus. Lively and tripping.

Then, children, sing away, O, sing away, away! For there in heaven you shall sing and shine;

Then, children, sing away, O, sing away, away! For there in heaven you shall sing and shine;

Then, children, sing away, O, sing away, away! For there in heaven you shall sing and shine.

Then, children, sing away, O, sing away, away! For there in heaven you shall sing and shine.

May be sung as a Quartette to the Chorus.

SWEET EVENING HOUR.

Words by G. W. HINSDALE. Music by W. H. DOANE.

1. How dear to me the twilight hour, When Je - sus draws me with his love;
2. The spir - it whis-pers in my ear, When the first shad - ow falls at eve,

When earth's at-trac-tions lose their power, And I can soar to joys a - bove.
Leave earthly friends, for I am near, With the best gifts thou canst re - ceive.

Sweet evening hour! the day is done, The noi - sy day, with all its care,
The Sav-ior draws me with his love, And soothes my heart, o'erwhelmed with care;

And I can sit with God a - lone, And seek his face in humble prayer.
His gen - tle voice my grief removes, He takes my hand, he hears my prayer.

Chorus.

Sweet evening hour! sweet evening hour! When Je - sus draws me with his love;

Ritard.

Sweet evening hour! sweet evening hour! When Je-sus draws me with his love.

MARCHING ON!

Published by the AMERICAN BAPTIST SOCIETY. Words and Music by REV. R. LOWRY.

1. Marching on! marching on! glad as birds on the wing, Come the bright ranks of chil-dren from near and from far; Hap - py hearts, full of song, 'neath our ban - ners we bring, Lit - tle sol - diers of Zi - on pre - pared for the war.
2. Press-ing on! press-ing on! to the din of the fray, With the firm tread of faith to the bat - tle we go; 'Mid the cheer - ing of an - gels, our ranks march a-way, With our flags point-ing ev - er right on t'wards the foe.
3. Fight-ing on! fight-ing on! in the midst of the strife, At the call of our Cap - tain, we draw ev' - ry sword; We are bat - tling for God, we are struggling for life, Let us strike ev' - ry reb - el that fights 'gainst the Lord.
4. Sing - ing on! sing - ing on! from the bat - tle we come, Ev' - ry flag bears a wreath, every sol - dier re - nown; Heavenly an - gels are wait - ing to wel - come us home, And the Sav - ior will give us a robe and a crown.

Chorus.

March-ing on! march-ing on! sound the bat - tle cry! sound the bat - tle cry!
For the Sav - ior is be - fore us, And for Him we draw the sword.
Marching on! marching on! shout the vic - to - ry! shout the vic - to - ry!
We will end the bat - tle sing - ing hal - le - lu - jahs to the Lord.

GOING HOME.

Inscribed to Mrs. M. Barstow, Plainfield, Conn.

Words by Miss J. C. Ringwood. Music by W. H. Doane.

1. We're going to a happy home, Going home, going home; To join with those before us gone,
2. O! peaceful is that blessed shore, Going home, going home; Where ills of life afflict no more,
3. We're going, O, what joys arise! Going home, going home; Hopes of that blissful par-a-dise,
Going home, going home. To clasp again in fond embrace The loved ones of that happy place, And
Going home, going home. The sorrowing pilgrim finds release, The weary rest in perfect peace, And
Going home, going home. Then let our feeble bodies die, We have a mansion in the sky, We'll
Chorus.
see our Sav-ior face to face, Go-ing home, go-ing home. Go-ing home, go-ing home,
pain and death for - ev - er cease, Go-ing home, go-ing home. Go-ing home, go-ing home,
glad - ly shout when death is nigh, Go-ing home, go-ing home. Go-ing home, go-ing home,
Yes, we're going home; We'll gladly shout when death draws near, We're going, going home.
Yes, we're going home; We'll gladly shout when death draws near, We're going, going home.

TRUST IN JESUS.

"Looking unto Jesus, the author and finisher of our faith."—*Heb.* xii: 2.

Words from S. S. TIMES. W. H. D.

1. Christian! is thy path-way dreary? Is thy heart oppressed with fear?
Jesus calls the weak and weary, Makes them objects of his care.
Listen to his invitation; He is waiting to release;
In the hour of tribulation, He will give thee "perfect peace."

2. Jesus saw thee in thy blindness, Guilty, wretched, far from God,
And in sovereign love and kindness, Saved thee through his precious blood.
Still, thy helplessness confessing, To his care thy all resign;
He will send his heavenly blessing, Gently whisper, "Thou art mine."

3. Christian! wherefore yield to sadness? Fix thy heart and hopes above;
Look to Jesus—and with gladness, Trust his gracious, pard'ning love;
Trials here will sorely press thee, Let thy trust on him be stayed;
He will cheer and guide, and bless thee, With his ever-present aid.

4. Think how kind, how condescending! Jesus calls himself thy "Friend,"
From his throne in glory bending, He will every prayer attend.
He will never, never leave thee, Through thy pilgrim days below;
Then, at last, he will receive thee, And a crown of life bestow.

Chorus.

Whisper, whisper ever-blessed Jesus, Gently whisper
whisper, "Thou art mine."

FIRST TIME. SECOND TIME.

"THE GOOD SHIP ZION."

Words by Rev. A. A. Graley. Music by W. H. Doane.

1. We are homeward bound to the land of light and love; With a swelling sail we onward sweep;
2. Though the billows rise, they shall never overwhelm, Though the breakers roar upon the lea;

3. Though for ages past she has plowed the stormy main, She 's the stout ship Zion as of yore;
4. Ho, ye youthful souls, there is danger in your path, By the chart of folly you 're mis-led;
5. We are homeward bound; won't you join our happy crew? Come aboard, poor sinner, while you may;

Though the rude winds blow, there is One who rules above, Who will guard the weary sailor on the deep.
'Mid the strife we 'll sing, for we 've Jesus at the helm, And he 'll steer the good ship Zion o'er the sea.

Safe 'mid rocks and shoals, and the fearful hurricane, She has thousands brought to Canaan's happy shore.
There are rocks beneath, and above a storm of wrath, And the breakers of destruction are ahead.
To the eye of faith there 's the better land in view, 'T is the land that shines with never-ending day.

Chorus.

In the good ship Zi-on we are tossing on the tide, But the wild dark tempest soon shall cease;

In the good ship Zi-on we are tossing on the tide, But the wild dark tempest soon shall cease;

All the danger o-ver, she will safe at anchor ride, In the port of ev - er - lasting peace.

All the danger o-ver, she will safe at anchor ride, In the port of ev - er - lasting peace.

THE LAND OVER JORDAN.

W. H. DOANE.

1. There is a land of pure de - light, Where saints im-mor - tal reign;
2. There ev - er - last - ing spring a - bides, And nev - er - with'ring flowers;
3. Sweet fields be - yond the swell - ing flood Stand dressed in liv - ing green;
4. O, could we make our doubts re-move, Those gloomy doubts that rise,
5. Could we but climb where Mo - ses stood, And view the landscape o'er,
In - fi - nite day ex - cludes the night, And pleasures ban - ish pain.
Death, like a nar - row sea di - vides This heavenly land from ours.
So to the Jews old Ca - naan stood, While Jor - dan rolled be - tween.
And view the Ca - naan that we love, With un - be - cloud - ed eyes.
Not Jor - dan's stream nor death's cold flood Should fright us from the shore.
Chorus
O! the land, the love - ly land, The land o - ver Jor - dan's foam; On the
O! the land, the love - ly land, The land o - ver Jor - dan's foam; On the
1st time. | 2d time.
golden, golden strand Wait the happy, happy band, To welcome the ransomed home.
golden, golden strand Wait the happy, happy band, To welcome the ransomed home.

DENNIS.

NAGELI.

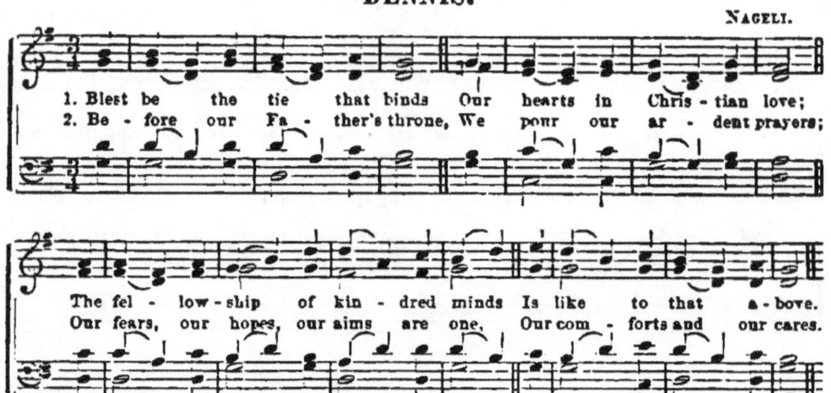
1. Blest be the tie that binds Our hearts in Chris - tian love;
2. Be - fore our Fa - ther's throne, We pour our ar - dent prayers;
The fel - low - ship of kin - dred minds Is like to that a - bove.
Our fears, our hopes, our aims are one, Our com - forts and our cares.

3 We share our mutual woes,
Our mutual burdens bear;
And often for each other flows,
The sympathizing tear.

4 When we asunder part,
It gives us inward pain;
But we shall still be joined in heart,
And hope to meet again.

CORONATION. C. M.

HOLDEN.

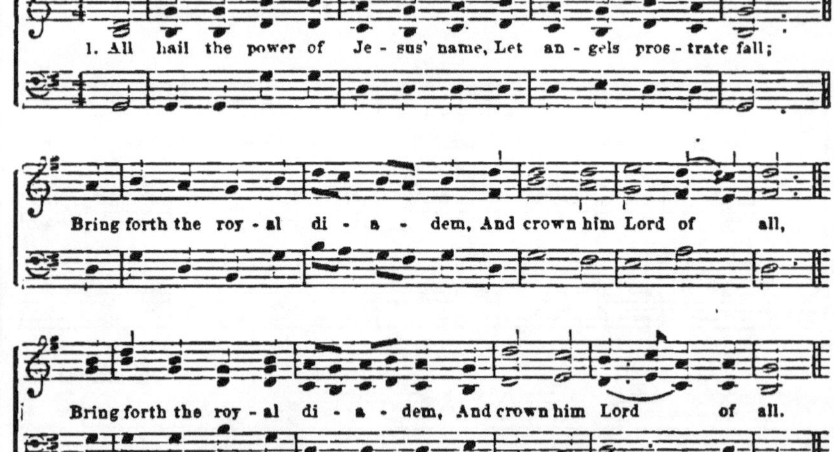
All Sing.
1. All hail the power of Je - sus' name, Let an - gels pros - trate fall;
Bring forth the roy - al di - a - dem, And crown him Lord of all,
Bring forth the roy - al di - a - dem, And crown him Lord of all.

2 You chosen seed of Israel's race,
A remnant weak and small,
Hail him who saves you by his grace,
And crown him Lord of all.

3 You Gentile sinners, ne'er forget
The wormwood and the gall;
Go, spread your trophies at his feet,
And crown him Lord of all.

4 Let every kindred, every tribe,
On this terrestrial ball,
To him all majesty ascribe,
And crown him Lord of all.

5 O, that with yonder sacred throng,
We at his feet may fall!
We'll join the everlasting song,
And crown him Lord of all.

WE 'LL WAIT TILL JESUS COMES.

Duet or Quartette.
Full Chorus.
1. My heavenly home is bright and fair, We'll be gathered home;
2. Its glittering towers the sun out-shine, We'll be gathered home;
3. My Father's house is built on high, We'll be gathered home;
4. When from this earth-ly pris-on free, We'll be gathered home;
Duet or Quartette.
Full Chorus.
Nor death nor sigh-ing vis-it there, We'll be gath-ered home.
That heaven-ly man-sion shall be mine, We'll be gath-ered home.
A-bove the arched and star-ry sky, We'll be gath-ered home.
That heaven-ly man-sion shall be mine, We'll be gath-ered home.
Chorus.
We'll wait till Je-sus comes, We'll wait till Je-sus comes,
We'll wait till Je-sus comes, We'll wait till Je-sus comes,
We'll wait till Je-sus comes, And we'll be gath-ered home.
We'll wait till Je-sus comes, And we'll be gath-ered home.

BEAUTIFUL RIVER.

From "HAPPY VOICES," by permission. REV. R. LOWRY.

1. Shall we gath-er at the riv - er, Where bright an - gel feet have trod,
2. On the mar-gin of the riv - er, Wash - ing up its sil - ver spray,

3. Ere we reach the shining riv - er, Lay we ev' - ry bur-den down;
4. At the smiling of the riv - er, Mir - ror of the Savior's face,
5. Soon we'll reach the sil-ver riv - er; Soon our pil-grim-age will cease;

With its crys-tal tide for - ev - er Flowing by the throne of God?
We will walk and worship ev - er, All the hap - py, gold - en day.

Grace our spir - its will de - liv - er, And pro - vide a robe and crown.
Saints whom death will never sev - er, Lift their songs of sav - ing grace.
Soon our hap-py hearts will quiv - er With the mel - o - dy of peace.

Chorus.

p

Yes, we'll gath-er at the riv - er, The beau-ti-ful, the beau-ti-ful riv - er,

Yes, we'll gath-er at the riv - er, The beau-ti-ful, the beau-ti - ful riv - er,

Gath-er with the saints at the riv - er That flows by the throne of God.

Gath-er with the saints at the riv - er That flows by the throne of God.

BLESSED HOPE OF HEAVEN.

Most cordially inscribed to H. THANE MILLER, ESQ., by the Author.

Words by JOHN GOULDING.
W. H. DOANE.
1. How hap-py, hap-py ev - ery child of grace, Who knows and feels his sins forgiv'n;
This fleeting, fleet-ing earth is not my home! I seek a bet-ter home in heaven:
2. O, what a sweet and bles-sed hope is ours, While here below on earth we stay;
We ev - er more than taste the heavenly powers, And an-te-date the sol - emn day.
A coun - try far from mor - tal sight, By faith a - bove I seem to
We feel the res - ur - rec - tion near— Our life in Christ a - bove con-
see: Yes; the heavenly land of rest, the saint's de - light, The
cealed, And with his pre - cious, pre - cious pres-ence here, Our
Chorus.
land a - bove, prepared for me. May we all share, May we all share,
earthen ves - sels all are filled. May we, etc.
May we all share the bles-sed hope of heaven, Yes, the bles-sed, bles-sed hope, when
days and years are gone, We all may meet a - bove in heaven.

NONE BUT JESUS.

Written expressly for "The Little Sunbeam," by Rev. ROB'T LOWRY.

1. Weeping will not save me— Tho' my face were bathed in tears, That could not allay my fears, Could not wash the sins of years; Weeping will not save me.
2. Working will not save me— Purest deeds that I can do, Holiest thoughts and feelings too, Can not form my soul a-new; Working will not save me.
3. Waiting will not save me— Helpless, guilty, lost I lie, In my ears is mercy's cry, If I wait I can but die; Waiting will not save me.
4. Faith in Christ *will* save me— Let me trust thy weeping son, Trust the work that he has done, To his arms, Lord, help me run; Faith in Christ *will* save me.
Chorus.
Je-sus wept and died for me; Je-sus suf-fered on the tree;
Je-sus waits to make me free; He a-lone can save me!

LET IT PASS.

W. H. DOANE.

Soft and Sprightly.
f
pp
1. Be not swift to take offense, Let it pass, Let it pass; An - ger is a
2. Strife corrodes the pu - rest mind, Let it pass, Let it pass; As the un - re-
3. Ech - o not an an - gry word, Let it pass, Let it pass; Think how oft - en
4. Bid your an - ger to de - part, Let it pass, Let it pass; Lay those homely
f
foe to sense, Let it pass, Let it pass. Brood not darkly o'er a wrong,
gard-ed wind, Let it pass, Let it pass. An - y vulgar souls that live,
Duet, ad lib.
you have erred, Let it pass, Let it pass. Since our joys must pass a - way,
words to heart, Let it pass, Let it pass. Fol - low not the gid - dy throng,
Chorus.
Which will dis - ap-pear ere long; Brood not dark - ly o'er a wrong, Which will dis-ap-
May con-demn with-out reprieve; 'T is the no - ble who for-give, 'T is the no - ble
Like the dewdrop on the spray; Wherefore should our sorrows stay, Wherefore should our
Better to be wronged than wrong; Better to be wronged than wrong, Therefore sing this
pear ere long, Rath-er sing this cheer - y song, Let it pass, Let it pass.
who for-give; Rath-er sing this cheer - y song, Let it pass, Let it pass.
sor - rows stay; Rath-er sing this cheer - y song, Let it pass, Let it pass.
cheer-y song; Therefore sing this cheer - y song, Let it pass, Let it pass.

JUST ON THE OTHER SHORE.

To F. V. CHAMBERLAIN, Esq., Superintendent of Third Presbyterian Church Sabbath School, this little song is most cordially inscribed.

Words by SYDNEY DYER. W. H. DOANE.

1. O'er dark and storm-y wa - ters, A drear - y voyage I make, Where
2. Be - neath the mad-dened sur-ges, Deep plunging, down I go, When

3. A - wear - y, worn with toss - ing, When will my voyag - ing cease, And
4. Through murk and mist impending, The hap - py port is seen, A

thunders loudly bel - low, And lightnings flash and quake; Yet 'mid the howl - ing
yawn the watery ter - rors, To fear-ful depths be - low; But when, in dread - ful

give me in the har - bor, A home of end-less peace? I see the bliss - ful
speck beyond the surg-es, That wildly dash be - tween; And drift - ing, ev - er

tempest, A - bove the dash and roar, I see the bea - con glimmer, Just
pois-ing, I hang the break-ers o'er, A ra - diance still is beaming, Just

ha - ven Be - yond the wa - t'ry roar, Where glow the fields of E - den, Just
drift-ing, Still near - er than be - fore, I greet the bless - ed Ai - denn, Just

on the oth-er shore, I see the bea - con glimmer, Just on the oth-er shore.
on the oth-er shore, A ra-diance still is beaming, Just on the oth-er shore.

on the oth-er shore, Where glow the fields of Eden, Just on the oth-er shore.
on the oth-er shore, I greet the bless-ed Ai-denn, Just on the oth-er shore.

5 Ah, plainer now, and nearer,
'T is Beulah's cloudless land!
The place to cast my anchor,
A gold and pearly strand;
And just above, a mansion
With ever-open door,
Invites the weary voyager,
Just on the other shore.

6 Ah! nearer, gladly nearer,
With slackened, tattered sail,
I move through calmer waters;
The tempests cease to wail;
My anchor now is ready—
Anon I cast it o'er,
Forever sure and steadfast;
Just on the other shore.

"WHAT SHALL THE HARVEST BE?"

W. H. DOANE.

Marching time.

1. They are sowing their seed in the daylight fair; They are sow - ing seed in the
2. They are sowing their seed of word and deed, Which the cold know not, nor the

3. Some are sow-ing the seed of no - ble deed, With a sleepless watch, and an
4. And there's many yet standing with i - dle hands, Still they're scattering seed through-
5. Whether sown in the darkness or sown in light; Whether sown in weakness or

noon-day's glare; They are sow - ing seed in the soft twi - light; They are
care - less heed; O! the gen - tle word, and the kind - est deed, That have

earn - est heed; With a cease - less hand in the earth they sow, And the
out the land, And some who are sow - ing the seeds of care, Which their
sown in might; Whether sown in meek - ness or sown in wrath, In the

sow - ing their seed in the sol - emn night. What shall the har - vest be?
blest the sad heart in its sor - est need. Sweet shall the har - vest be;

Chorus.

fields are all whitening where'er they go. Rich will the har - vest be; - - -
soil long has borne, and it still must bear. Sad will the har - vest be; - - -
broad-est highway or the shadowy path. Sure will the har - vest be; - - -

Repeat softly.

What shall the harvest be? - - What shall the harvest be? What shall the harvest be?
Sweet shall the harvest be; - - Sweet shall the harvest be; Sweet shall the harvest be.

Rich will the harvest be; - - Rich will the harvest be; Rich will the harvest be.
Sad will the harvest be; - - Sad will the harvest be; Sad will the harvest be.
Sure will the harvest be; - - Sure will the harvest be; Sure will the harvest be.

SHALL I BE THERE?

Words by Wm. S. Kain. W. H. Doane.

1. There is a land, a beanteous land, Where ransomed saints for - ev - er stand,
2. Shall I those glo - ries e'er be - hold, Those pearly gates and streets of gold?
3. That glorious land when shall I see? O! is that blessed place for me?
4. When - e'er my wand'rings here shall cease, Re - ceive me in - to per - fect peace,
And songs of rap - ture fill the air, O, tell me, Lord, shall I be there?
And crowns of glo - ry shall I wear? O, tell me, Lord, shall I be there?
Is there a crown for me to wear? Shall I indeed, O Lord, be there?
And may thy voice to me de - clare, O, yes, my child, thou shalt be there!
Chorus.
Shall I be there? Shall I be there? O, tell me, Lord, shall I be there, And in those songs of
[Chorus to 4th verse.]
Thou shalt be there! Thou shalt be there! A crown of glory thou shalt wear, And in those songs of
rapture share? O, tell me, Lord, shall I be there? Shall I be there? Shall I be there?
rapture share! O, yes, my child, thou shalt be there! Thou shalt be there! Thou shalt be there!

TAKE A BLESSING WHILE WE LINGER.

W. H. DOANE.

1. Take a bless-ing, take a bless-ing, Ere we jour-ney on our way; Take a
2. May the peace of heav-en ev - er At your hearth and board re - main; May the
blessing while we lin - ger Where we long would gladly stay; 'T is the spir - it's ben - e-
gentlest breez-es waft you O - ver life's un - cer-tain main. Take a bless-ing while we
dic - tion, While the tear-drops free - ly start; Take the bless - ing, take the
lin - ger, Where we long would glad - ly stay; Take the bless - ing, take the
bless-ing, As it gushes from the heart, As it gush-es from the heart.
bless-ing, Ere we jour-ney on our way, Ere we jour-ney on our way.

3 Yes! these meetings and these partings
Will be over by and by,
When the loved and lost shall gather
At our Father's house on high;
Take a blessing, while we linger,
Where we long would gladly stay,
Take a blessing, take a blessing,
Ere we journey on our way.

THE WAY TO HEAVEN.

"JESUS SAITH UNTO HIM, I AM THE WAY

Words by Mrs. H. E. BROWN. W. H. DOANE.

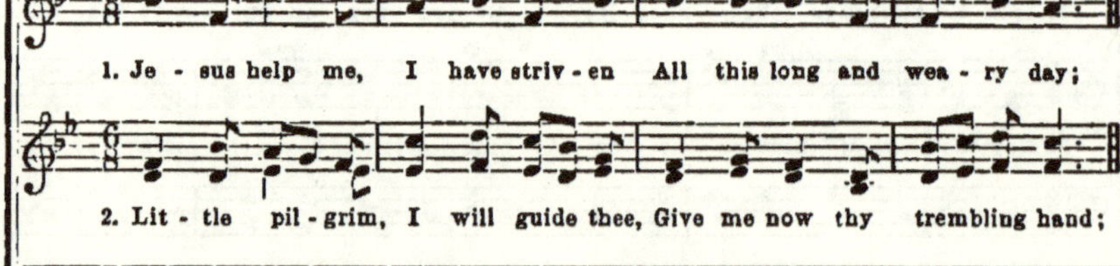

1. Je - sus help me, I have striv - en All this long and wea - ry day;

2. Lit - tle pil - grim, I will guide thee, Give me now thy trembling hand;

3. See this cross, all pierced and go - ry, When my life for thine was given;

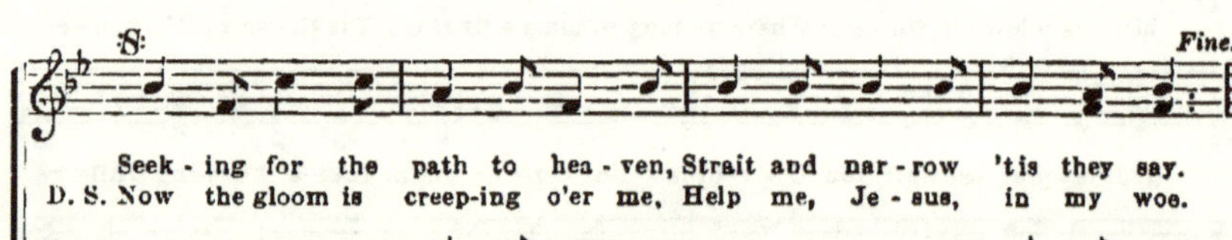

Fine.

Seek - ing for the path to hea - ven, Strait and nar - row 'tis they say.
D. S. Now the gloom is creep-ing o'er me, Help me, Je - sus, in my woe.

With my pres-ence close be - side thee, Thou shalt reach the wished-for land.
D. S. I can weep-ing souls de - liv - er, Whom God's broken law would slay.

O'er this lies the path to glo - ry, 'T is the nar - row way to heaven.
D. S. With my pres - ence close be - side thee, Thou shalt reach the wished-for land.

D. S.

Quick! I turn, but, lo! be - fore me Tur - bid wa - ters dark - ly flow;

I can span that cru - el riv - er, With a new and liv - ing way;

Lit - tle pil - grim, I will guide thee, Give me now thy trembling hand;

PILGRIM. 8s.

1 GENTLY, Lord, O! gently lead us
Through this lonely vale of tears;
Through the changes thou 'st decreed us,
Till our last great change appears.
When temptation's darts assail us,
When in devious paths we stray,
Let thy goodness never fail us,
Lead us in thy perfect way.

2 In the hour of pain and anguish,
In the hour when death draws near,
Suffer not our hearts to languish,
Suffer not our souls to fear;
And, when mortal life is ended,
Bid us on thy bosom rest,
Till by angel bands attended,
We awake among the blest.

THERE'LL BE NO PARTING THERE.

W. H. DOANE.

Slow and gliding.
1. Here we meet to part a - gain; Here we meet to part a - gain; But
2. Here we meet to part a - gain; Here we meet to part a - gain; But
3. Here we meet to part a - gain; Here we meet to part a - gain; But
4. Here we meet to part a - gain; Here we meet to part a - gain; But
when we meet on Canaan's plain, There 'll be no parting there, In that bright world a-
when a seat in heaven we gain, There 'll be no parting there, In that bright world a-
there we shall with Je - sus reign, There 'll be no parting there, In that bright world a-
when we join the heavenly train, There 'll be no parting there, In that bright world a-
Chorus.
bove, In that bright world a - bove. Shout! shout the victo - ry! We 're on our journey
bove, In that bright world a - bove. Shout, etc.
bove, In that bright world a - bove. Shout! shout the victo - ry! We 're on our journey
bove, In that bright world a - bove. Shout, etc.
home; Shout! shout the vic - to - ry! We're on our jour - ney home.
home; Shout! shout the vic - to - ry! We're on our jour - ney home.

BEAR THY CROSS CHEERFULLY.

W. H. DOANE.

Gently.
1. Bear thy cross cheer - ful - ly, Broth-er, the night Pas - seth though
2. Bear it with white hands up, Sis - ter in pain, Drinking life's
3. Thro' the surging sor - row's tide, Vales dark and lone, Up the steep
4. Bear thy cross trust-ing - ly, Whate'er it be, Then will it
tear - ful - ly, Dim is thy sight; Car - ry it du - teous-ly,
bit - terest cup, Know 't is in vain; Hope-ful - ly, prayerful - ly,
mountain's side, Mak - ing no moan, Tho' thou 'rt shrinking weari - ly
ten - der - ly Rest up - on thee; Think not to lay it down
Look-ing a - far, Where now gleams beau-teous-ly, The morn - ing
Light then 't will be, For the Lord care - ful - ly Thus lead - eth
Be - neath the load, Take it up cheer-i - ly, 'T is from thy
Till life is done— For the cross shall wear the crown When heaven is
star, Where now gleams beau-teous-ly The morn - ing star.
thee, For the Lord care - ful - ly, Thus lead - - eth thee.
God, Take it up cheer-i - ly, 'T is from thy God.
won, For the cross shall wear the crown, When heaven is won.

COME, COME TO THE SAVIOR.

1. Come, come, come to the Sav - ior, Rich, rich mer - cy re - ceive;
2. Come, come, la - den and wea - ry, Christ, Christ calls thee to come;
3. Come, come, seek his sal - va - tion, Now, now hear and o - bey;
4. Hark! hark! an - gels are sing - ing, Love, love, love is their theme;

Here, here you will find par - don, Je - sus from sin will re - lieve.
Leave, leave paths dark and drea - ry, Cease from the Sav - ior to roam.
Hark! hark! th' sweet in - vi - ta - tion, An - gels in - vite you a - way.
Peace, peace, joy - ful - ly bring - ing, Mer - cy from God, the Su - preme.

Come, come, come, come, Come to the Sav - ior and live.
Come, come, come, come, Je - sus will guide thee safe home.
Come, come, come, come, Sin - ner, be - lieve and o - bey.
Come, come, come, come, Je - sus is rich to re - deem.

GOD IS LOVE! I KNOW, I FEEL.

W. H. ROBERTS.

Moderato Legato. *Chorus, faster. Staccato.*

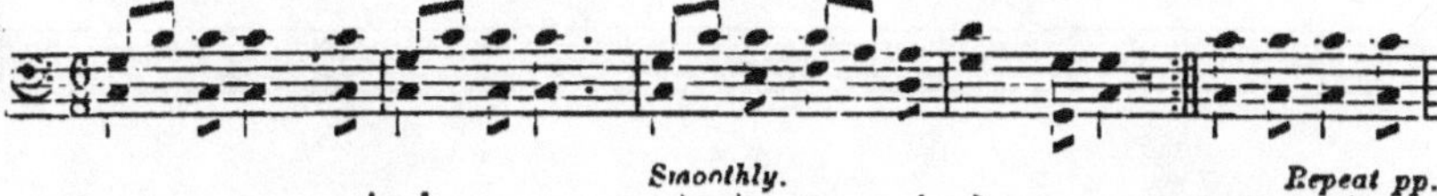

1. Depth of mer - cy, can there be Mer - cy still reserved for me? } God is love! I
Can my God his wrath forbear, Me, the chief of sinners, spare? }

2. I have long withstood his grace; Long provoked him to his face; } God is love, etc.
Would not hearken to his calls; Grieved him by a thousand falls. }

Smoothly. *Repeat pp.*

know, I feel; Jesus weeps and loves me still; Je - sus weeps, he weeps and loves me still.

2 Now incline me to repent;
Let me now my sins lament;
Now my foul revolt deplore,
Weep, believe, and sin no more.
God is love, etc.

4 There for me the Savior stands;
Shows his wounds, and spreads his hands;
God is love! I know, I feel,
Jesus weeps and loves me still.
God is love, etc.

THE CHILDREN'S WELCOME.

W. H. DOANE.

Sprightly.
1. We have come rejoicing on this happy day, In our Sunday-school we dearly love to stay;
2. Thro' the week he's kept us, and his smiling face Still is beaming on us in this happy place;
3. Jesus there is smiling on his Father's throne, Saying, Come in, welcome, come, for here is room;
4. And in robes of glory, like the stars above, Shall my loved ones ever, ever with me rove;
And with voi-ces blending in a sa-cred song, We the Sav-ior's praise prolong.
And the gracious Spir - it from his ho - ly throne, Tells us of a bet - ter home.
In these shining mansions, I have still a place; Children, has - ten to my face.
Where the waving flowerets of im - mortal bloom, Shed a - round their sweet perfume.
Chorus.
There we shall nev - er grieve him more, But with the an - gels on that shore,
There we shall nev - er grieve him more, But with the an - gels on that shore,
f
Strike the harps of glory in a sweeter strain, And ev - er with them praise his holy name.
Strike the harps of glory in a sweeter strain, And ev - er with them praise his holy name.

"GO AND SOW."

W. H. Doane.

Andante—Legato.
1. Go and sow be - side all wa - ter, In the morn - ing of thy
youth; In the eve - ning scat - ter broad-cast, Pre - cious seeds of liv - ing
truth; For tho' much may sink and per - ish In the rock - y, bar - ren
mold, And the har - vest of thy la - bor, May be less than thir - ty
fold, May be less than thir - - ty fold;

2 Let thy hand be not withholden,
Still beside all waters sow—
For thou knowest not which shall prosper—
Whether this or that shall grow;
While some precious portions scattered,
Germinating, taking root,
Shall spring up and grow and riben
Into never-dying fruit.

3 Therefore, sow beside all water,
Trusting—hoping—toiling on,
When the fields are white for harvest,
God will send his angels down;
And thy soul may see the value
Of its patient morns and eves,
When the everlasting garner
Shall be filled with precious sheaves.

"ONE DAY NEARER HOME."

W. H. DOANE.

1. O'er the hills the sun is set - ting, And the eve is draw-ing on;
2. Worn and wea - ry oft the pil - grim Hails the set - ting of the sun;
3. Near-er home! yes, one day near - er To our Fa - ther's house on high;
4. "One day near - er," sings the mari - ner, As he glides the waters o'er;
Slow - ly drops the gen - tle twi - light, For an - oth - er day is gone.
For the goal is one day near - er, And his jour - ney near - ly done.
To the green fields and the foun - tains Of the land be - yond the sky.
While his light is soft - ly dy - ing On his dis - tant, na - tive shore.
Gone for aye, its race is o - ver, Soon the darker shades will come; Still 't is sweet to
Thus we feel when o'er life's desert, Heart and sandal sore we roam; As the twilight
For the heaven's grow brighter o'er us, And the lamps hang in the dome; And our tents are
Thus the Christian on life's ocean, As his light-boat cuts the foam, In the evening
know at e - ven, We are one day nearer home, We are one day nearer home.
gath - ers o'er us, We are one day nearer home, We are one day nearer home.
pitched still closer, For we 're one day nearer home, For we re one day nearer home.
cries with rapture, "I am one day nearer home," "I am one day nearer home."

NOTE.—The first eight measures may be sung as a Quartette, with good effect, if desired.

"LET ME GO."

1. Let me go, the day is breaking, Dear compan-ions, let me go;
2. Let me go: I may not tar-ry, Writhing though with doubt and fears;
We have spent a night of wak-ing, In this wil-der-ness of woe.
An-gels wait my soul to car-ry, Where my kin-dred, Lord, ap-pears.
Chorus.
1st. 2d.
Up-ward now I wend my way, Part we here at break of day.
Friends and kin-dred weep not so; If you love me let me go.

3 We have traveled long together,
Hand in hand and heart in heart.
Both through fair and stormy weather,
And 't is hard, 't is hard to part.
While I sigh farewell to you,
Answer, one and all, "Adieu."

4 'T is not darkness gathering round me,
That withdraws me from your sight;
Walls of earth no more can bind me,
But, translated into light,
Like the lark, on mountain wing,
Though unseen, you hear me sing.

5 Heaven's broad day hath o'er me broken,
Far beyond earth's span of sky!
Am I dead! Nay; by this token,
Know that I have ceased to die;
Would you solve the mystery?
Come up hither, come and see.

ON TO VICTORY.

W. H. D.

1. Saints for whom the Savior bled, In your Captain's footsteps tread, Follow Jesus and be led
2. Christian soldier on with me, Soon your en-emies must flee; Your reward before you see,
3. By the ransom which he gave, By his triumph o'er the grave, Trust his mighty power to save;
On to vic - to - ry! See your foeman take the ground, While the signal trumpet sounds,
Sparkling from on high! Boldly take the glorious field, You may fall, but must not yield,
Firm and faithful be. And when death's dark hour is nigh, When the tear-drop dims the eye,
Chorus.
Hear his accents pour around Cheering mel - o - dy. Come to Je - sus, come to
You shall write upon your shield, Vict'ry, tho' you die. Come to Je - sus, come to
You shall in the parting sigh Grasp the vic - to - ry. Come to Je - sus, etc.
Je - sus, He will write up - on thy brow, Vic - to - ry, vic - to - ry, vic - to - ry.
Je - sus, He will write up - on thy brow, Vic - to - ry, vic - to - ry, vic - to - ry.

HE LEADETH ME.

Inscribed to W. E. London, of Third Presbyterian Church Sabbath-school, Cin., O.

W. H. DOANE.

1. He lead - eth me, O, blessed thought! O, words with heavenly comfort fraught!
2. Sometimes 'mid scenes of deep - est gloom; Sometimes where Eden's bow - ers bloom;
3. Lord, I would clasp thy hand in mine, Nor ev - er murmur or re - pine;
4. And when my task on earth is done; When, by thy grace, the victory's won,
What-e'er I do, where-e'er I be, Still 't is God's hand that lead - eth me!
By wa - ters still, o'er troubled sea, Still 't is his hand that lead - eth me!
Con - tent, what-ev - er lot I see, Since 't is my God that lead - eth me!
E'en death's cold wave I will not flee, Since God through Jordan lead - eth me!
Chorus.
He leadeth me, leadeth me, lead - eth me; By his own hand he leadeth me,
He leadeth me, leadeth me, lead - eth me; By his own hand he leadeth me,
leadeth me; His faithful follower I would be, For by his hand he leadeth me.
leadeth me; His faithful follower I would be, For by his hand he leadeth me.

"FAR AWAY."

Contributed to the "Little Sunbeam" by R. Lowry.

1. There is a home where all is bright, Far a - way, far a - way,
There is no dark and stormy night, Far a - way, far a - way.
For Je - sus said, I will pre - pare The child of God a man - sion
fair; O! may I have a dwell-ing there, Far a - way, far a - way.

2 Then let the storm be wild and long,
Jesus loves; Jesus loves;
And this shall be my daily song,
Jesus loves; Jesus loves.
He loves, he loves; I know, I feel,
Young as I am, he loves me still;
O, may I do his blessed will!
Jesus loves; Jesus loves.

3 And then at home I soon shall be,
Far away, far away;
From care and pain shall soon be free,
Far away, far away.
For tears of grief are never known
In that bright world I call my own;
And swiftly I am passing on,
Far away, far away.

"O, WASH ME IN THY PRECIOUS BLOOD."

Words by H. Bonar. W. H. Doane.

1\. A few more years shall roll, A few more sea - sons come, And
2\. A few more storms shall beat On this wild rock - y shore, And

we shall be with those that rest, A - sleep within the tomb. Then O, my Lord, pre-
we shall be where tem - pests cease, And surges swell no more. Then O, my Lord, pre-

pare My soul for that great day; O! wash me in thy
pare My soul for that calm day; O! wash me in thy

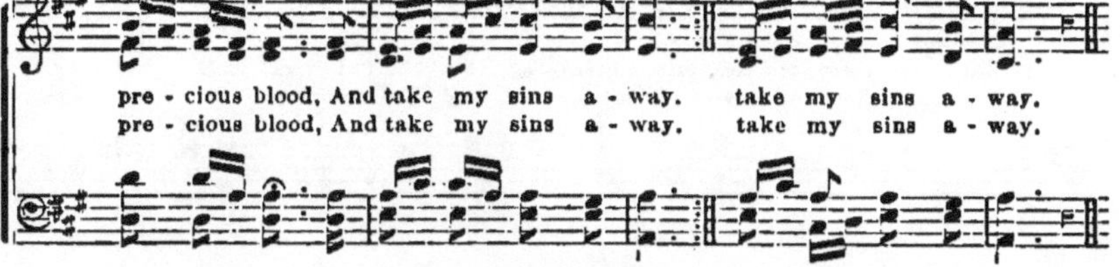
FIRST TIME.
SECOND TIME.
pre - cious blood, And take my sins a - way. take my sins a - way.
pre - cious blood, And take my sins a - way. take my sins a - way.

3 A few more Sabbaths here,
Shall cheer us on our way,
And we shall reach the endless rest,
Th' eternal Sabbath day.
Then O, my Lord, prepare
My soul for that sweet day;
O! wash me in thy precious blood,
And take my sins away.

4 'T is but a little while,
And he shall come again,
Who died that we might live, who lives
That we with him might reign.
Then O, my Lord, prepare
My soul for that glad day;
O! wash me in thy precious blood,
And take my sins away.

"WAITING, ONLY WAITING."

W. H. DOANE.

1. On - ly wait - ing till the shad-ows Are a lit - tle lon - ger grown,
2. On - ly wait - ing till the reap - ers Have the last sheaf gath-ered home:

On - ly wait - ing till the glim - mer Of the day's last beam is flown,
For the sum-mer time is fa - ded, And the au - tumn winds have come.

☞ Solo for Tenor, or Tenor and Alto, or may be sung as a Quartet.

Till the night of earth is fa - ded From the heart once full of day—
Quick-ly, reap-ers, quick-ly gath - er The last ripe hours of my heart,

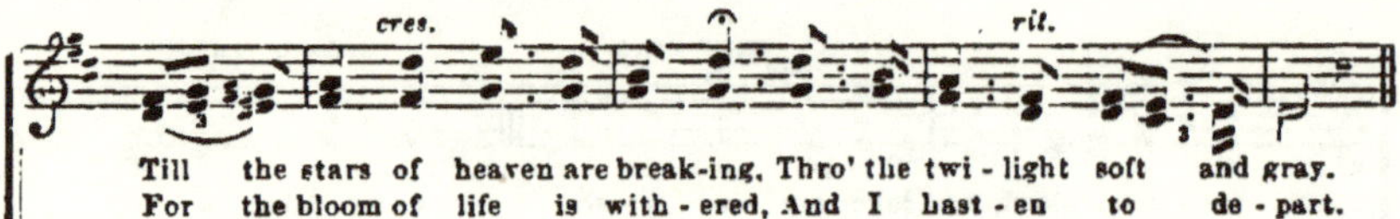

Till the stars of heaven are break-ing, Thro' the twi - light soft and gray.
For the bloom of life is with - ered, And I hast - en to de - part.

Chorus.

Waiting, waiting, waiting till the shadow's
Waiting, waiting, waiting till the shadows are a little longer grown.

3 Only waiting till the angels
Open wide the mystic gate,
At whose feet I long have lingered,
Weary, poor and desolate.
Even now I hear their footsteps,
And their voices, far away,
If they call me I am waiting,
Only waiting to obey.

4 Only waiting till the shadows
Are a little longer grown,
Only waiting till the glimmer
Of the day's last beam is done;
Then from out the gathering darkness
Holy, deathless stars arise,
By whose light my soul shall gladly,
Tread its pathway to the skies.

PRAISE TO JESUS.

Words by Rev. James Lisk. Music by W. H. Doane.

Spirited.
1st time. 2d time.
1. Je - sus is our King and Sa - vior, Let us praise his glo-rious name,
Join in one triumph-al cho - rus, Wide to spread his - - - truth and fame;
Come, and let us all ex - alt him, While be - fore his throne we sing,
Je - sus is our King and Sa - vior, We to him our prais-es bring.
Chorus.
Who would not sing praise to Je - sus? For he died up - on the cross to save;
Died to of - fer all sal - va - tion free, Hope in death, and vict'ry o'er the grave.

2 Let the children all adore him,
Round his cross their anthem swell;
Fill the air with hallelujahs,
While his grace and love they tell.
Shout his name to every people,
Wheresoe'er the sun doth shine,
Let the dark, benighted pagans,
In our song their voice combine.
Who would not, etc.

3 Now upon his throne of glory,
Yet for us he intercedes,
Pointing to the wounds he still bears,
Ever now for sinners pleads.
Let us all, then, sing his praises,
For he is our Friend and King,
He will not forsake us ever,
While we love his praise to sing.
Who would not, etc.

JESUS IS OUR SHEPHERD.

W. H. DOANE.

1. Je - sus is our shep - herd, Wip - ing ev - ery tear;

Fold - ed in his bo - som, What have we to fear?

On - ly let us fol - low, Whith-er he doth lead—

To the thirst - y des - ert, Or the dew - y mead.

2 Jesus is our shepherd;
  Well we know his voice—
How its gentlest whisper
  Makes our hearts rejoice;
Even when he chideth,
  Tender is his tone;
None but he shall guide us—
  We are his alone.

3 Jesus is our shepherd;
  For the sheep he bled,
Every lamb is sprinkled
  With the blood he shed.
When we tread death's valley,
  Dark with fearful gloom,
We will fear no evil,
  Victors o'er the tomb.

MY HEAVENLY HOME.

1. My heavenly home is bright and fair; Nor pain nor death can en - ter there;
Its glittering towers the sun out-shine; That heavenly mansion shall be mine.

Chorus.
I'm go - ing home, I'm go - ing home, I'm go - ing home to die no more.

2 My Father's house is built on high,
Far, far above the starry sky:
When from this earthly prison free,
That heavenly mansion mine shall be.
I'm going home, etc.

3 Let others seek a home below,
Which flames devour, or waves o'erflow;
Be mine a happier lot to own
A heavenly mansion near the throne.
I'm going home, etc.

JESUS! LOVER OF MY SOUL.

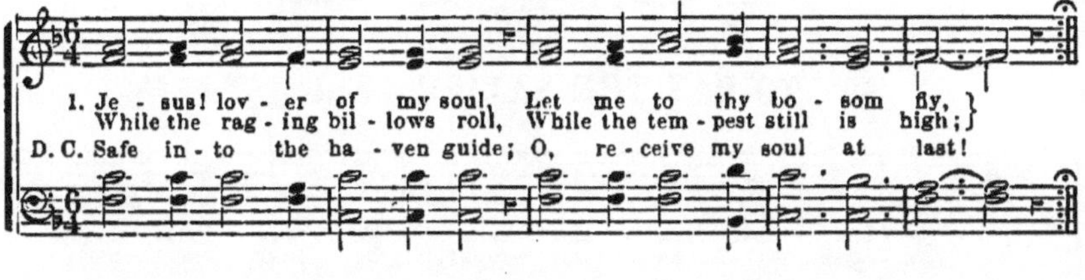
1. Je - sus! lov - er of my soul, Let me to thy bo - som fly,
While the rag - ing bil - lows roll, While the tem - pest still is high;
D. C. Safe in - to the ha - ven guide; O, re - ceive my soul at last!

D. C.
Hide me, O! my Sa - vior, hide, Till the storm of life is past;
D. C.

2 Other refuge have I none—
Hangs my helpless soul on thee!
Leave, ah! leave me not alone!
Still support and comfort me.
All my trust on thee is stayed;
All my help from thee I bring;
Cover my defenseless head
With the shadow of thy wing.

2 Thou, O Christ, art all I want;
All and all in thee I find;
Raise the fallen, cheer the faint,
Heal the sick, and lead the blind;
Just and holy is thy name,
I am all unrighteousness;
Vile, and full of sin, I am,
Thou art full of truth and grace.

WHEN SHALL WE MEET AGAIN?

DR. L. MASON.

1. When shall we meet a - gain, Meet ne'er to sev - er? When will peace
2. When shall love free-ly flow, Pure as life's riv - er? When shall sweet
3. Up to that world of light, Take us, dear Sa - vior; May we all

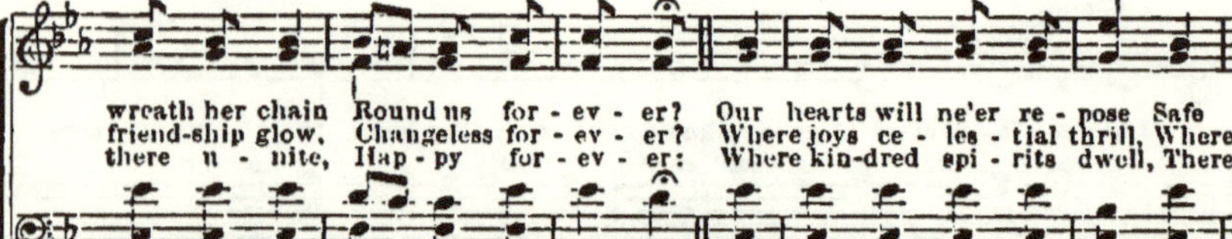
wreath her chain Round us for - ev - er? Our hearts will ne'er re - pose Safe
friend-ship glow, Changeless for - ev - er? Where joys ce - les - tial thrill, Where
there u - nite, Hap - py for - ev - er: Where kin-dred spi - rits dwell, There

from each blast that blows In this dark vale of woes— Nev-er—no, nev-er.
bliss each heart shall fill, And fears of part-ing chill Nev-er—no, nev-er.
may our mu - sic swell, And time our joys dis - pel, Nev-er—no, nev-er.

TO-DAY THE SAVIOR CALLS.

1. To - day the Sa - vior calls; Ye wan - d'rers come;
2. To - day the Sa - vior calls; O, hear him now;

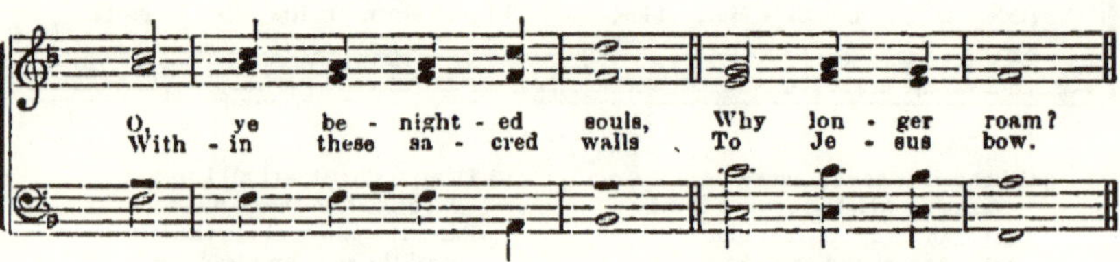
O, ye be - night - ed souls, Why lon - ger roam?
With - in these sa - cred walls To Je - sus bow.

3 To-day the Savior calls;
For refuge fly;
The storm of justice falls,
And death is nigh.

4 The Spirit calls to-day;
Yield to his power;
O, grieve him not away;
'T is mercy's hour.

MY FAITH LOOKS UP TO THEE.

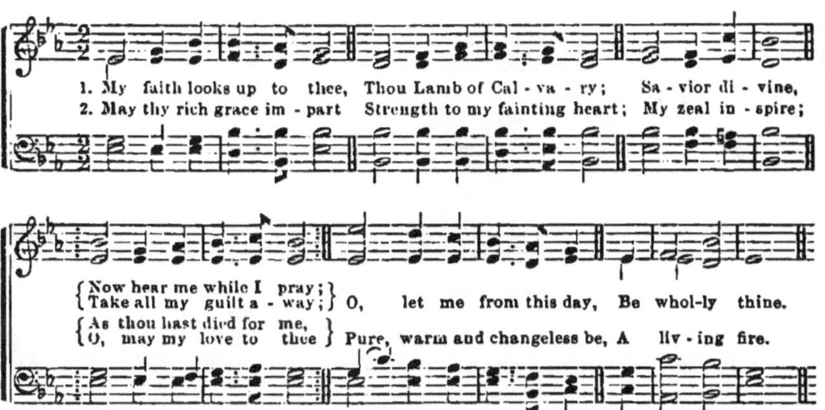
1. My faith looks up to thee, Thou Lamb of Cal - va - ry; Sa - vior di - vine,
2. May thy rich grace im - part Strength to my fainting heart; My zeal in - spire;
{Now hear me while I pray; Take all my guilt a - way;} O, let me from this day, Be whol-ly thine.
{As thou hast died for me, O, may my love to thee} Pure, warm and changeless be, A liv - ing fire.

3 While life's dark maze I tread,
And griefs around me spread,
Be thou my guide;
Bid darkness turn to day,
Wipe sorrow's tears away,
Nor let me ever stray
From thee aside.

4 When ends life's transient dream,
When death's cold, sullen stream
Shall o'er me roll,
Blest Savior, then, in love,
Fear and distress remove,
O, bear me safe above,
A ransomed soul.

BOYLSTON. S. M.

Dr. L. Mason.

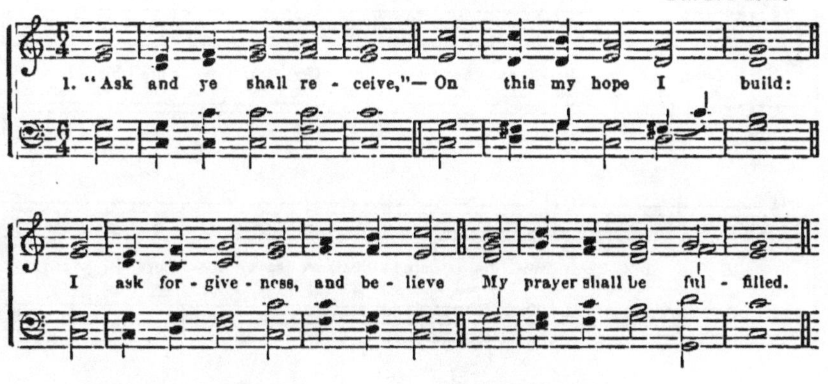
1. "Ask and ye shall re - ceive,"— On this my hope I build:
I ask for - give - ness, and be - lieve My prayer shall be ful - filled.

3 Seek and expect to find:
Wounded to death in soul,
I seek the Savior of mankind,
For he can make me whole.

3 Knock, and with patience wait,
By faith free entrance gain:
I stand and knock at mercy's gate
Till I thy grace obtain.

4 Shall I then ask in vain?
Seek, and not find the Lord?
Knock, and yet no admittance gain
And doubt thy holy Word?

5 No, Lord, thou 'lt ne'er deceive;
Thy promises are sure;
In thy good time I shall receive;
What can I ask for more?

MY SOUL BE ON THY GUARD.

DR. L. MASON.

1. My soul, be on thy guard; Ten thou-sand foes a - rise:
The hosts of sin are press-ing hard To draw thee from the skies.

2 O, watch and fight and pray;
The battle ne'er give o'er;
Renew it boldly every day,
And help divine implore.

3 Ne'er think the victory won,
Nor lay thine armor down;
Thy arduous work will not be done
Till thou obtain thy crown.

4 Fight on, my soul, till death
Shall bring thee to thy God;
He'll take thee at thy parting breath,
To his divine abode.

PLEYEL'S HYMN.

J. PLEYEL.

1. Lord, we come be - fore thee now— At thy feet we hum - bly bow;
O, do not our suit dis - dain! Shall we seek thee, Lord, in vain?

2 Lord, on thee our souls depend;
In compassion now descend;
Fill our hearts with thy rich grace,
Tune our lips to sing thy praise.

3 In thy own appointed way,
Now we seek thee, here we stay;
Lord, we know not how to go,
Till a blessing thou bestow.

4 Send some message from thy word,
That may peace and joy afford;
Let thy Spirit now impart
Full salvation to each heart.

JESUS MY ALL.
mf
p
mf
1. Lord, at thy mer - cy - seat, Hum - bly I fall; Pleading thy
2. Tears of re - pent - ant grief Si - lent - ly fall; Help thou my
3. Hark! how the words of love Ten - der - ly fall, Ere to the
4. Still at thy mer - cy - seat, Hum - bly I fall; Pleading thy
p
promise sweet, Lord, hear my call. Now let thy work be-gin, O, make me
un - be-lief, Hear thou my call. O, how I pine for thee, 'T is all my
realms a-bove, Heard is my call. Now every doubt has flown, Broken my
promise sweet, Heard is my call. Faith wings my soul to thee, This all my
p
pure with-in, Cleanse me from ev'-ry sin, Je - sus, my all.
hope, my plea. Je - sus has died for me, Je - sus, my all.
heart of stone, Lord, I am thine a - lone, Je - sus, my all.
hope shall be, Je - sus has died for me, Je - sus, my all.
THE LORD'S PRAYER. (Chant.)
W. H. DOANE.
Slow and distinct, in exact time.
1. Our Father, who art in heaven, hallowed | be thy | name; Thy kingdom come; thy will be done on | earth, as it | is in | heaven. Amen.
2. Give us this day our | daily | bread; And forgive us our trespasses, as we forgive | them that | trespass a- | gainst us.
3. And lead us not into temptation, but deliver | us from | evil; For thine is the kingdom, and the power, and the | glory, for | ever and | ever. Amen.

I WILL ARISE.

DUET AND QUARTETTE.
Arr. by W. H. DOANE.
Andante, ad lib.
p
I will a - rise, I will a - rise, and go to my Father, and will
I will a - rise, I will a - rise, and go to my Father, and will
p mp mf dim.
say un-to him, Fa - ther, Fa - ther, Father, I have sinned, I have
say un-to him, Fa - ther. Fa - ther, Father, I have sinned, I have
p
sinned against heaven, and before thee, and before thee, and am no more
sinned against heaven, and before thee, and before thee, and am no more
pp
worthy to be call-ed thy son, To be call - - - - ed thy son.
worthy to be call-ed thy son, To be call - - - - - - - - - - - ed thy son.

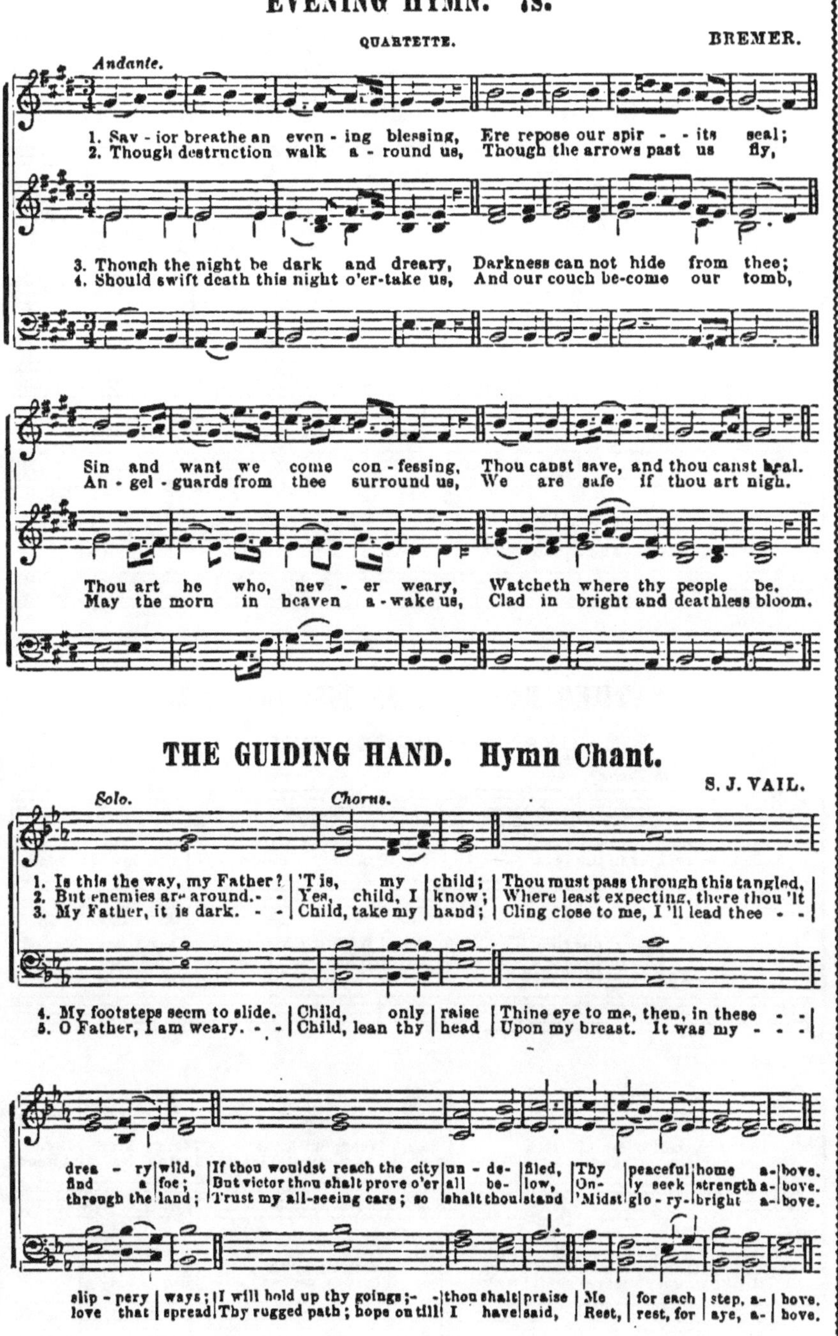
EVENING HYMN. 7s.
QUARTETTE.
BREMER.
Andante.
1. Sav - ior breathe an even - ing blessing, Ere repose our spir - - its seal;
2. Though destruction walk a - round us, Though the arrows past us fly,
3. Though the night be dark and dreary, Darkness can not hide from thee;
4. Should swift death this night o'er-take us, And our couch be-come our tomb,
Sin and want we come con - fessing, Thou canst save, and thou canst heal.
An - gel - guards from thee surround us, We are safe if thou art nigh.
Thou art he who, nev - er weary, Watcheth where thy people be.
May the morn in heaven a - wake us, Clad in bright and deathless bloom.
THE GUIDING HAND. Hymn Chant.
S. J. VAIL.
Solo.
Chorus.
1. Is this the way, my Father? | 'T is, my | child; | Thou must pass through this tangled,
2. But enemies are around. - - | Yes, child, I | know; | Where least expecting, there thou 'lt
3. My Father, it is dark. - - | Child, take my | hand; | Cling close to me, I 'll lead thee - -
4. My footsteps seem to slide. | Child, only | raise | Thine eye to me, then, in these - -
5. O Father, I am weary. - - | Child, lean thy | head | Upon my breast. It was my - - -
drea - ry | wild, | If thou wouldst reach the city | un - de- | filed, | Thy | peaceful | home a- | bove.
find a | foe; | But victor thou shalt prove o'er | all be- | low, | On- | ly seek | strength a- | bove.
through the | land; | Trust my all-seeing care; so | shalt thou | stand | 'Midst | glo - ry- | bright a- | bove.
slip - pery | ways; | I will hold up thy goings;- - | thou shalt | praise | Me | for each | step, a- | bove.
love that | spread | Thy rugged path; hope on till | I have | said, | Rest, | rest, for | aye, a- | bove.

60
JESUS GUIDE.
Words by JAMES UPHAM.
Music by W. H. DOANE.
1. The way is dark; | I can not see at all. | My Je - sus guide, My Je - sus guide!
2. The way is rough; | my feet are ver-y sore. | My Je - sus, aid, My Je - sus, aid!
3. The way affrights; | fierce foemen lurk around. | My Je - sus, save, My Je - sus, save!
4. The way is long; | I fear I yet may fail. | My Je - sus, keep, My Je - sus, save!
5. The way—it ends! | the ra - diant gate appears! | My Je - sus fast, My Je - sus fast!
O, let me feel | the clasping of thy hand | Close by my side, Close by my side.
O, let me lean, | while yet thou lead-est on, | Nor me upbraid, Nor me up-braid.
O, let me cling, | and hide my-self in thee, | While demons rave, While demons rave.
O, let my faith | out-last the weary road, | No more to weep, No more to weep!
My spirit hastes | and bounds with joy, to be | At home at last, At home at last!
FATHER ROCK US IN THY CRADLE.
CHANT FOR CHILDREN.
W. H. D.
Softly, with Feeling.
1. Father, rock us in thy | cra - - - | dle, | We, thy little - - | chil - dren | pray;
2. Father, rock us in thy | cra - - - | dle, | And above each - - | pil - lowed | head,
3. Kiss us ere we sleep, our | Fa - - - | ther, | With thy kiss of - | par - don | blessed;
4. Father, rock us in thy | cra - - - | dle, | When our day of - | life is | done;
5. Then, O Father, softly | rock - - | us | In the cradle - - - | of thy | love.
In the hush of eve we | seek - - - | thee, | Weary with the - - | long, long | day.
Like a curtain, soft and | shad - - | owy, | Let thy watchful - | wing be | spread.
And through all the still night | watch- | es, | Give us each thy - | prom - ised | rest.
When the gathering shades have | dark- | ly, | Shut away the - - | gold - en | sun;
Till our wondering eyes shall | wak- - | en, | On thy perfect - - | day a- | bove.

THE LORD IS MY SHEPHERD.

W. H. DOANE.

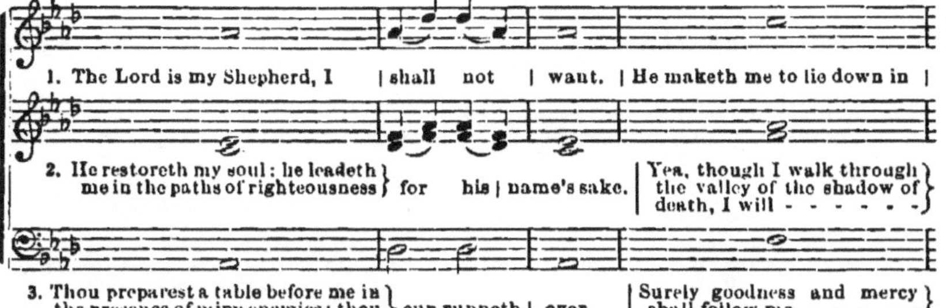
1. The Lord is my Shepherd, I | shall not | want. | He maketh me to lie down in |
2. He restoreth my soul: he leadeth me in the paths of righteousness for his | name's sake. | Yea, though I walk through the valley of the shadow of death, I will
3. Thou preparest a table before me in the presence of mine enemies: thou anointest my head with oil; my cup runneth | over. | Surely goodness and mercy shall follow me

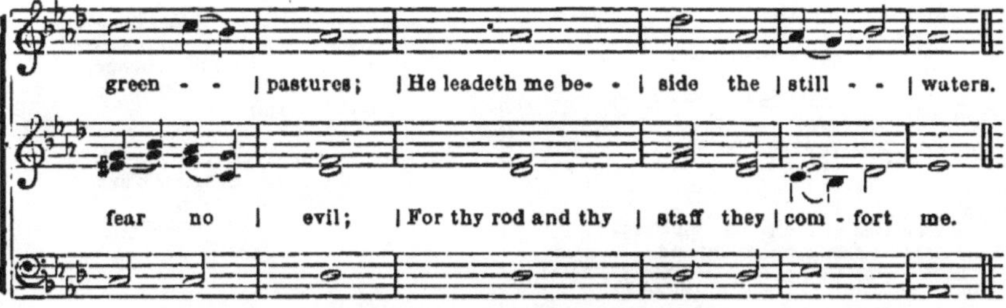
green - - | pastures; | He leadeth me be- - | side the | still - - | waters.
fear no | evil; | For thy rod and thy | staff they | com - fort me.
all the | days of my life; | And I will dwell in the | house of the | Lord for- | ever.

MARY AT THE SAVIOR'S CROSS.

W. H. DOANE.

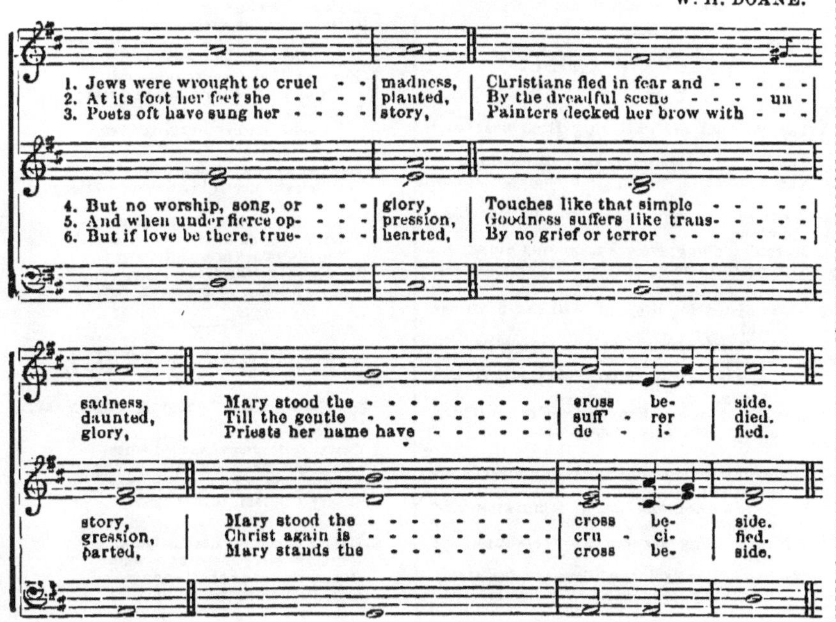
1. Jews were wrought to cruel - - | madness, | Christians fled in fear and - - - - - |
2. At its foot her feet she - - - - | planted, | By the dreadful scene - - - - un - |
3. Poets oft have sung her - - - - | story, | Painters decked her brow with - - - |
4. But no worship, song, or - - - | glory, | Touches like that simple - - - - - |
5. And when under fierce op- - - - | pression, | Goodness suffers like trans- - - - - |
6. But if love be there, true- - - - | hearted, | By no grief or terror - - - - - - |
sadness, | Mary stood the - - - - - - - - - - | cross be- | side.
daunted, | Till the gentle - - - - - - - - - - | suff' - rer | died.
glory, | Priests her name have - - - - - - | de - i- | fied.
story, | Mary stood the - - - - - - - - - - | cross be- | side.
gression, | Christ again is - - - - - - - - - - | cru - ci- | fied.
parted, | Mary stands the - - - - - - - - - - | cross be- | side.

NEVER BE AFRAID.

Key F.

1 Never be afraid to speak for Jesus,
Think how much a word can do;
Never be afraid to own your Savior,
He who loves and cares for you.

CHORUS.

Never be afraid, never be afraid,
Never, never, never,
Jesus is your loving Savior,
Therefore never be afraid.

2 Never be afraid to work for Jesus,
In His Vineyard day by day,
Labor with a kind and willing spirit,
He will all your toil repay.
Never be afraid, &c.

3 Never be afraid to bear for Jesus,
Keen reproaches when they fall;
Patiently endure your every trial,
Jesus meekly bore them all.
Never be afraid, &c.

4 Never be afraid to live for Jesus;
If you on his care depend.
Safely shall you pass through every trial,
He will bring you to the end.
Never be afraid, &c.

5 Never be afraid to die for Jesus;
He the life, the truth, the way,
Gently in his arms of love will bear you
To the realms of endless day.
Never be afraid, &c.

MARCHING ALONG.

Key C.

1 The children are gath'ring from near and from far,
The trumpet is sounding the call for the war,
The conflict is raging 'twill be fearful and long,
We'll gird on our armor and be marching along.
Marching along, we are marching along,
Gird on the armor, and be marching along.

2 We've listed for life, and will camp on the field;
With Christ as our Captain, we never will yield;
The "sword of the Spirit," both trusty and strong,
We'll hold in our hands as we're marching along. Marching along, etc.

3 Through conflicts and trials our crowns we must win,
For here we contend 'gainst temptation and sin;
But one thing assures us, we cannot go wrong,
If trusting our Savior, while marching along.
Marching along, etc.

A HOME BEYOND THE TIDE.

Key E♭.

1 We are out on the ocean sailing,
Homeward bound we sweetly glide;
We are out on the ocean sailing
To a home beyond the tide.

All the storms will soon be over,
Then we'll anchor in the harbor;
We are out on the ocean sailing,
To a home beyond the tide;
We are out on the ocean sailing,
To a home beyond the tide.

2 Come on board, O! "ship" for glory,
Be in haste—make up your mind!
For our vessel's weighing anchor,
You will soon be left behind!
All the storms, etc.

3 When we all are safely anchored,
We will shout—our trials o'er!
We will walk about the city,
And we'll sing forevermore.
All the storms, etc.

MARY TO THE SAVIOR'S TOMB.

TUNE—"Martyn." Key F. 7s. Double.

1 MARY to the Savior's tomb
Hasted at the early dawn;
Spice she brought and sweet perfume,
But the Lord she loved had gone.
For awhile she lingering stood,
Filled with sorrow and surprise;
Trembling while a crystal flood
Issued from her weeping eyes.

2 But her sorrows quickly fled,
When she heard his welcome voice;
Christ has risen from the dead,
Now he bid her heart rejoice.
What a change his word can make,
Turning darkness into day;
Ye who weep for Jesus' sake,
He will wipe your tears away.

INVITATION OF CHRIST.

TUNE.—"Horton." Key A. 5th P. M.

1 COME, saith Jesus' sacred voice,
Come and make my paths your choice;
I will guide you to your homes;
Weary Pilgrim, hither come.

2 Hither come, for here is found
Balm for every bleeding wound,
Peace, that ever shall endure,
Rest eternal, sacred, sure.

FAR OUT UPON THE PRAIRIE.

Key B♭. 7s & 6s.

1 Far out upon the prairie,
How many children dwell,
Who never read the Bible,
Or hear the Sabbath bell;
And when the holy morning
Wakes us to sing and pray,
They spend the precious moments
In idleness and play.

CHORUS.

Far out upon the prairie,
How many children dwell,
Who never read the Bible,
Or hear the Sabbath bell.

2 For they have no kind pastor,
Whose loving words have told
Of Jesus, the Good Shepherd,
And called them to his fold;
No Sabbath-school inviting
Its pleasant doors within,
No teacher's voice entreating
To leave the way of sin.
Far out, etc.

A LIGHT IN THE WINDOW.

Key A♭.

1 THERE'S a light in the window for thee, brother,
There's a light in the window for thee;
A dear one has moved to the mansions above,
There's a light in the window for thee.

CHORUS.

A mansion in heaven we see,
And a light in the window for thee;
A mansion in heaven we see,
And a light in the window for thee.

2 There's a crown, and a robe and a palm, brother,
When from toil and from care you are free;
The Savior has gone to prepare you a home,
With a light in the window for thee.
A mansion in heaven, etc.

3 O watch, and be faithful, and pray, brother,
All your journey o'er life's troubled sea;
Though afflictions assail you, and storms beat severe,
There's a light in the window for thee.
A mansion in heaven, etc.

4 Then on, perseveringly on, brother,
Till from conflict and suffering free,
Bright angels now beckon you over the stream,
There's a light in the window for thee.
A mansion in heaven, etc.

THE SUNDAY SCHOOL.

Key A. C. M.

1 The Sunday-school that blessed place,
Oh! I would rather stay
Within its walls a child of grace,
Than spend my hours in play.

CHORUS.

The Sunday-school, the Sunday-school,
Oh! 'tis the place I love;
For there I learn the golden rule,
Which leads to joys above.

2 'Tis there I learn that Jesus died
For sinners such as I;
Oh! what has all the world beside,
That I should prize so high.
The Sunday-school, etc.

3 Then let our grateful tribute rise,
And songs of praise be given
To Him who dwells above the skies,
For such a blessing given.
The Sunday-school, etc.

4 And welcome, then, the Sunday school,
We'll read and sing and pray,
That we may keep the golden rule,
And never from it stray.
The Sunday-school, etc.

THE PROMISED LAND.

Old Tune. Key E♭.

1 I have a Father in the promised land,
I have a Father in the promised land;
My Father calls me, I must go
To meet him in the promised land.

CHORUS.

I'll away, I'll away to the promised land,
I'll away, I'll away to the promised land,
My Father calls me I must go
To meet Him in the promised land.

2 I have a Savior in the promised land,
I have a Savior in the promised land;
My Savior calls me, I must go
To meet Him in the promised land.
I'll away, etc.

3 I have a crown in the promised land,
I have a crown in the promised land;
When Jesus calls me, I must go
To wear it in the promised land.
I'll away, etc.

4 I hope to meet you in the promised land,
I hope to meet you in the promised land;
At Jesus' feet, a joyous band,
We'll praise Him in the promised land.
We'll away, etc.

I'M A PILGRIM.

Key G.

1 I'm a pilgrim, and I'm a stranger,
I can tarry, I can tarry but a night;
Do not detain me, for I am going
To where the streamlets are ever flowing.
I'm a pilgrim, and I'm a stranger,
I can tarry, I can tarry but a night.

2 There the sunbeams are ever shining,
I am longing, I am longing for the sight;
Within a country unknown and dreary,
I have been wandering forlorn and weary.
I'm a pilgrim, etc.

3 Of that country to which I'm going,
My Redeemer, my Redeemer is the light;
There are no sorrows, nor any sighing,
Nor any sin there, nor any dying.
I'm a pilgrim, etc.

JESUS LOVES ME.

Key E♭.

1 Jesus loves me! this I know,
For the Bible tells me so,
Little ones to him belong,
They are weak, but he is strong.

CHORUS.

Yes, Jesus loves me,
Yes, Jesus loves me,
Yes, Jesus loves me,
The Bible tells me so.

2 Jesus loves me! he who died,
Heaven's gate to open wide;
He will wash away my sins,
Let His little child come in.
Chorus.

3 Jesus loves me! loves me still,
Though I'm very weak and ill,
From His shining throne on high,
Comes to watch me where I lie.
Chorus.

4 Jesus loves me! He will stay
Close beside me, all the way
If I love Him, when I die
He will take me home on high.
Chorus. Jesus loves me, &c.

THE BLOOD OF CHRIST.

TUNE—"Fountain." C. M.

1 There is a fountain filled with blood,
Drawn from Immanuel's veins,
And sinners plunged beneath that flood
Lose all their guilty stains.

2 The dying thief rejoiced to see
That fountain in his day;
And there may I, as vile as he,
Wash all my sins away.

3 Dear dying Lamb, thy precious blood
Shall never lose its power,
Till all the ransomed church of God
Be saved to sin no more.

4 E'er since, by faith, I saw the stream
Thy flowing wounds supply,
Redeeming love has been my theme,
And shall be till I die.

5 Then in a nobler, sweeter song,
I'll sing thy power to save,
When this poor lisping, stammering tongue
Lies silent in the grave.

TO-DAY THE SAVIOR CALLS.

Key F.

1 To-day the Savior calls!
Ye wand'rers come;
Oh, ye benighted souls!
Why longer roam!

2 To-day the Savior calls!
For refuge fly;
The storm of vengeance falls,
And death is nigh.

3 To-day the Savior calls!
Oh, hear him now!
Within these sacred walls
To Jesus bow.

4 The Spirit calls to-day!
Yield to his power;
Oh, grieve him not away,
'T is mercy's hour.

THE BRIGHT CROWN.

Key C.

1 Ye valiant soldiers of the Cross,
Ye happy, praying band,
Though in this world you suffer loss,
You'll reach fair Canaan's land.

CHORUS.

Let us never mind the scoffs nor the frowns of the world.
For we've all got the cross to bear;
It will only make the crown the brighter to shine,
When we have the crown to wear.

2 All earthly pleasures we'll forsake,
When Heaven appears in view,
In Jesus' strength we'll undertake
To fight our passage through.
Let us never, etc.

3 O what a glorious shout there'll be,
When we arrive at home!
Our friends and Jesus we shall see,
And God shall say, "Well done."
Let us never, etc.

I'M BUT A STRANGER HERE.

W. H. DOANE.

Slow and gliding.
1. I'm but a stran - ger here, Heaven is my home;
Earth is a des - ert drear, Heaven is my home;
Dan - ger and sor - row stand Round me on ev - ery hand,
Heaven is my fa - ther - land— Heaven is my home.

2 What though the tempest rage?
  Heaven is my home;
Short is my pilgrimage,
  Heaven is my home;
Time's cold and wintry blast
Soon will be overpast,
Heaven is my fatherland,
  Heaven is my home.

3 There at my Savior's side,
  Heaven is my home;
I shall be glorified,
  Heaven is my home;
There are the good and blest,
There, too, I soon shall rest,
Heaven is my fatherland,
  Heaven is my home.

"IN THAT HAPPY LAND."

May be sung as a Duet the first time. Arr. by W. H. Doane.

1. We are trav'-ling home to heaven a - bove, Will you go with us?
We are trav'-ling home to heaven a - bove, Will you go with us?
Chorus.
O, that's the heaven that I'm bound for, That's the heaven I love;
O, that's the heaven that I'm bound for, That's the heaven for me.

2 Dear companions will you go with us,
Will you go with us,
Dear companions will you go with us,
To that happy land?

3 Dear parents will you go with us,
Will you go with us,
Dear parents will you go with us,
To that happy land?

4 Let us meet, dear children, in that land,
In that happy land;
Let us meet, dear children, in that land,
In that happy land.

5 Let us meet, dear parents, in that land,
In that happy land;
Let us meet, dear parents, in that land,
In that happy land.

6 Our Savior he will lead us on,
Will you go with us?
Our Savior he will lead us on,
To that happy land.

COME TO JESUS.

1 Come to Jesus, come to Jesus now,
Come to Jesus now.

2 He will save you, he will save just now,
He will save just now.

3 Only trust him, only trust him now,
Only trust just now.

4 He is able, he is able now,
He is able now.

5 He is willing, he is willing now,
He is willing now.

6 He 'll forgive you, he 'll forgive just now,
He 'll forgive just now.

7 Flee to Jesus, flee to Jesus now,
Flee to Jesus now.

8 Jesus loves you, Jesus loves you now,
Jesus loves you now.

www.ingramcontent.com/pod-product-compliance
Lightning Source LLC
Chambersburg PA
CBHW021520090426
42739CB00007B/696

* 9 7 8 3 3 3 7 3 3 4 8 7 1 *